To Dan and Manecas.

I hope you will

enjoy reading

Love + light

Lesly.

INTUITION
AND
CHAKRAS

© Sheri Frrailick

About the Author

Lesley Phillips, PhD, is a spiritual teacher focused on helping people access their personal intuitive guidance. She has offered intuitive sessions and energy healing since 1996 and has taught meditation, healing, and intuition development since 2003. Dr. Lesley has provided spiritual guidance to thousands through her School of Intuition courses, Unlocking Your Truth radio show and podcast, books, mentoring sessions, workshops, readings, and healings.

She originally trained as an environmental microbiologist and searched tropical regions of the planet for natural product medicines. Later, she was a business negotiator for life science companies. She created her School of Intuition to bring teachings about intuition to as many people as possible. She believes that psychic senses are our most natural form of communication, and that as we evolve into an awakened species we will reclaim these abilities and use them as naturally as we now use our physical senses.

She created her signature Psychic Ability Blueprint chart and consultation to help her clients validate their unique purpose and remind them of the amazing potential of their intuitive abilities. She has created numerous online courses and workshops to help people master these gifts: from the foundational Unlock Your Intuition psychic development course, to courses on individual psychic senses such as clairvoyance, clairaudience, clairsentience, and claircognizance, to her advanced Kundalini mastery courses.

Dr. Lesley also creates automatic drawings that convey spiritual information. She created Portico Soul Essence Cards, a deck that opens the intuition and creativity of its users. She is author of a spiritual novel, *The Midas Tree,* which aims to help children keep, and adults remember, their spiritual gifts. She is happiest when working on her next creative project to support her mission to bring intuition to the mainstream.

For more information about her intuition development courses, to have your Psychic Ability Blueprint chart done, receive a reading or a healing, participate in a workshop, listen to podcasts, join her mailing list, download meditations, and discover other ways to connect with her, please visit https://drlesleyphillips.com/ or join her Awaken Your Intuition Facebook Group, https://www.facebook.com/groups/288011298447383/.

LESLEY PHILLIPS
PhD

INTUITION
AND
CHAKRAS

HOW TO
INCREASE
YOUR PSYCHIC
DEVELOPMENT
THROUGH
ENERGY

LLEWELLYN PUBLICATIONS
WOODBURY, MINNESOTA

FIRST EDITION
First Printing, 2020

Cover design by Shira Atakpu
Interior chakra figure by Mary Ann Zapalac

Llewellyn Publications is a registered trademark of Llewellyn Worldwide Ltd.

Library of Congress Cataloging-in-Publication Data
Names: Phillips, Lesley, author.
Title: Intuition and chakras : how to increase your psychic development
   through energy / Lesley Phillips, PhD.
Description: First edition. | Woodbury, Minnesota : Llewellyn Publications,
   2020. | Includes bibliographical references.
Identifiers: LCCN 2019055210 (print) | LCCN 2019055211 (ebook) | ISBN
   9780738762753 | ISBN 9780738763743 (ebook)
Subjects: LCSH: Psychic ability. | Intuition—Miscellanea. | Chakras.
Classification: LCC BF1031 .P49 2020 (print) | LCC BF1031 (ebook) | DDC
   131—dc23
LC record available at https://lccn.loc.gov/2019055210
LC ebook record available at https://lccn.loc.gov/2019055211

Llewellyn Worldwide Ltd. does not participate in, endorse, or have any authority or responsibility concerning private business transactions between our authors and the public.

All mail addressed to the author is forwarded but the publisher cannot, unless specifically instructed by the author, give out an address or phone number.

Any internet references contained in this work are current at publication time, but the publisher cannot guarantee that a specific location will continue to be maintained. Please refer to the publisher's website for links to authors' websites and other sources.

Llewellyn Publications
A Division of Llewellyn Worldwide Ltd.
2143 Wooddale Drive
Woodbury, MN 55125-2989
www.llewellyn.com

Printed in the United States of America

Other Books by Lesley Phillips, PhD

The Midas Tree (https://themidastree.com/)

Dedicated to all awakening humans
and our cocreation of a new planetary reality.

CONTENTS

Part Three
FIVE MEDITATION TECHNIQUES
FOR INTUITION DEVELOPMENT

EXERCISES AND MEDITATIONS

DISCLAIMER

This book is intended to provide educational information on topics related to metaphysics, spirituality, and personal and spiritual development. The author and publisher are not engaged in rendering legal, medical, financial, or other professional services. All suggestions offered by the author are complementary to the support offered by professionals, including, but not limited to, doctors, lawyers, healthcare practitioners, and financial advisers. The writings, meditations, and other exercises in this book provide a spiritual perspective. They are not intended to take the place of a medical diagnosis, doctor's consultation, treatment by the medical profession, legal advice, financial advice, or any other type of advice provided by a professional adviser.

Though unconfirmed by Western medicine, it is possible that the exercises in this book could lead to changes in your mental, emotional, and physical state as you release energy and integrate new information. By reading this book, you acknowledge this, read it at your own risk, and agree you will do the following:

- Operate from your own free will at all times.
- Not use the information in place of professional advice.
- Continue to follow the advice of your doctor and health professionals.
- Retain only what feels correct for you and leave the rest behind.
- Stop your meditation or exercise immediately if you feel uncomfortable.
- Consult with licensed professionals for your specific problems as appropriate.

- Take responsibility for your physical, emotional, mental, and spiritual health, including changes that occur during and after practicing the meditations and exercises in this book.

- Familiarize yourself with Dr. Lesley's training and credentials to understand what is being offered.

- Release author and publisher from all legal liability during and after receiving this information.

The methods presented in this book appear to result in positive outcomes. However, it's not possible to guarantee any specific results regarding your goals for using the techniques offered. This book is not intended to tell you what you should believe or do. The author believes in free will and your ability to make your own life choices. The author and publisher assume no liability or responsibility to any person or entity with respect to any loss or damage related directly or indirectly to the information in this book. No warranties of any kind, express or implied, are made. In consideration of the agreement to receive the information in this book, you agree to release and discharge and hold harmless the publisher, author, and their respective agents, heirs, assigns, contractors, and employees from any and all claims, demands, damages, rights of action or causes of action, present or future, arising out of or connected with your participation in the exercises in this book or which may occur as a result of following information within it. You acknowledge and agree that you assume the risks associated with any and all exercises in which you participate. If you don't wish to be bound by the above, you should not read this book.

ACKNOWLEDGMENTS

I am grateful for the ongoing support and encouragement of my partner, Corry Kouwenberg. Thanks also to Karilee Orchard for suggesting I write this book. It has been a journey involving significant personal growth and commitment, but ultimately has been very rewarding. Thank you to my friend Virginia Dudley for reading the book and validating it as being unique and really good. My appreciation also goes to Larna and Yumi for their monthly injections of clarity and support. Thanks also to my spiritual mentor, Mary Ellen Flora, for her honest feedback and encouragement.

I also wish to thank all of the readers of this book for being part of this magnificent co-creation, and my guides for helping me keep my energy clear enough to write it.

INTRODUCTION

Imagine asking your inner wisdom about your problems and receiving solutions you can rely on. Instead of being uncertain and asking friends what to do, envision receiving your own crystal-clear answers. Tapping into your intuition whenever you wish, being assured of answers to life's big questions, and following your trusted guidance to happiness and success are all within your reach. Whether you have questions about your life purpose, health or finances, or important decisions to make about relationships and career, this book will show you how to access your intuition and help you clear your uncertainty.

When asked how they would like their life to change by developing intuition, most people want to make better decisions for an easier life. They believe greater clarity will bring more peace, confidence, and happiness. They also mention physical, mental, emotional, and spiritual problems they hope intuition can solve. It is true that intuition can assist with all of these aspects of life. Intuition is the light that clarifies all things. When you can see yourself clearly and view your life honestly, you are empowered. Self-awareness lets you know what is in your way and how to change it. When you follow your intuition and your life improves, you become confident and open-hearted.

There are contrasting views on intuition. Skeptics demand tangible scientific evidence. Blind followers accept external guidance without discernment. Seekers hope it will unlock the mysteries of life and reveal their purpose. Believers know there is something in it as they have had direct personal experience. Masters use it like ordinary physical senses because to them it is as normal as breathing. Reading this book will expand your intuition knowledge no matter where you sit on the spiritual spectrum. It will help you not to ignore or misunderstand, but rather honor and treasure this gift. You will learn there are many ways to be intuitive. Instead of remaining elusive or fleeting, your intuitive senses can be mastered.

Simply put, intuition is your ability to understand something immediately without the need for conscious reasoning. Intuition can take many forms, including claircognizance, your sense of knowing; clairsentience, your gut feelings; clairaudience, intuitively hearing messages; and clairvoyance, your ability to see energy. Other forms include telepathy, precognition, and healing. We will cover them all. Learning to access your intuition can be very rewarding from a physical, emotional, mental, and spiritual perspective. The path to developing your intuition includes healing yourself, as you cannot receive or transmit a clear intuitive signal through a cloudy medium. The rewards of walking the intuitive path go beyond reading others. It will change your life completely.

Benefits of Intuition

Intuition can give you the freedom to help yourself and others. You can know why you are here and what choices will best bring you happiness and fulfillment. If you can access your intuition, then you can use it to illuminate your life path. You can know yourself more intimately and see others clearly. Connecting with your Trusted Source and accessing your higher guidance increases self-confidence, reduces doubt, and helps you release limiting beliefs. Being intuitive is empowering. You know what you want and can reclaim your energy and use it for you. Apart from this, your intuition allows you to communicate with the divine, angels, and guides. It lets you identify your life purpose and your special gifts. You can see auras and read past lives, listen to the music of the spheres, and know everything you need to love your life.

Relationships also improve or change in ways that enhance your life when you heal yourself and develop your intuition. You attract compatible people who are a match for the new you, leading to greater happiness and fulfillment. Following the intuitive path makes you more resilient to change and able to set clearer emotional boundaries. You can discern your energy from someone else's, detect interfering energy from others, and clear it out. If relationship questions prey on your mind and you wonder why you can't find a mate or if you should stay in a relationship, your intuition can answer them so you can make confident choices.

Developing your intuition trains you to be in charge of your body. You learn to calm emotions and quiet your mind. Then you, the spiritual consciousness, can direct your life. Being intuitive can enhance your mental focus, increase clarity, and lead to better judgment and memory recall. Your increased certainty will lead to improved decision-making. If you suffer from depression or mental anguish, you can alleviate it as you will know how to release its causes. You will appreciate the difference between your intellect, ego, and intuition. Doubt and confusion will go. Abundance and self-confidence will increase.

Intuition increases body awareness. You can listen to what your body needs to be a healthy, supportive partner on your life journey together. If you pay attention to your body, it fights you less and trusts you more. As meditation is used to develop intuition, you will be able to release your body's discomfort. It will relax. You might even sleep better. Once you are better rested, you probably will experience increased energy and improved health. If you do encounter health issues, you can rely on your intuition to provide information on healing, such as how to manage pain, adjust your diet, administer treatments, identify beneficial exercises, and improve your body systems.

If you are a worrier who lies awake at night concerned about money and career issues, or if you don't know why your abundance is blocked or why you always lose everything you have, intuition can help bring clarity and healing. Uncertainty on whether to accept a job offer, change careers, go back to school, or start your own business can be frustrating, but intuition can lead you to the solutions. Intuition helps you go with the flow and banish stress and anxiety. Your body talks to you through its emotions and physical symptoms. Listening with empathy and taking care of its needs puts you in balance, which in turn reduces stress. As intuition provides a clear perception of reality, you stop projecting and have less fear.

What Is in This Book

Intuition and Chakras will educate you about intuition and show you how it can answer your deepest questions. Intuition can help you lead a guided and purpose-filled life. This book will give you a foundation to open and develop it safely. There are three sections that take you on a journey of your intuitive senses.

Part One is all about you, your energy, and how to consciously create your life guided by intuition. Life can feel empty when you don't know who you are or why you are here. You might feel like a victim if you have no explanation for your pain. Your intuition can help you discover answers to the big questions and the small ones, including the one you probably have asked many times, "What is my life purpose?"

Knowing your purpose is not the same as consciously directing your life. For that, you must take charge of your energy field, as that is your creative universe. Harnessing your intuition provides awareness about what is in your energy field. Then you can release what you don't want and create what you do. You are spirit. You are not only your body. As an awakened human you must talk to and through your physical body. Your intuition is the path to doing this. In fact, intuition is spiritual communication and is how you communicate whether you're in a body or not. You interact with your body via spiritual centers called *chakras*. When you are not in resistance to life, energy flows easily through them, and you experience vitality. They also channel your intuitive senses and determine which types of extrasensory perception form your unique inner guidance system.

You'll also investigate what stops you from accessing your inner guidance and reaching your full potential. Intuition is demystified so it is accessible in your everyday life. You'll uncover seven commonly experienced blocks to intuition. Once you know them, you can observe them in your life and make changes so they no longer limit you. Then you'll bust some commonly held myths about intuition, so you can be free from unhelpful information. Whether picked up from friends, books, courses, or the internet, you will be able to release falsehoods and recognize what is correct for you. You'll also explore the main reasons for not acting on intuition and determine how well you currently follow your higher guidance. Once you bust the myths and overcome your blocks, you can reap the rewards of your intuition. You will align your personal goals for developing intuition with your greatest good, so you can benefit from following your higher guidance for the rest of your life.

Your profile of intuitive abilities is unique to you and encodes everything you need to fulfill your purpose. In Part Two, I will take you on a detailed tour of your intuitive guidance system. You'll also read about people who overcame their challenges and developed their intuition. As we journey through the types of intuition flowing through the sixth and seventh chakras, you will see how they connect you with higher frequencies and dimensions of reality. They allow you to communicate with your higher self, source energy, and other beings; as well as to observe the past, present, and future. Next, you'll explore the intuitive information flowing through the fifth chakra. It allows for a wide range of spiritual communication with other people and your guides. You'll also consider the hand chakras that are involved in manifesting. The sojourn continues with the intuitive abilities of the fourth, third, and second chakras. These centers connect you with your physical and astral bodies, humanity, and all creation as well as how you use your life force energy to create in these realities. You will learn how to tune in to your body's feedback.

Finally, you will focus on energy centers that help you navigate and manipulate energy in physical form. The first chakra and feet chakras connect you with physical reality and planet Earth. In addition, multiple chakras cooperate to sense and influence energy for balance, healing, and change. You will learn all about that as well.

In Part Three, you will learn foundational techniques to put you in charge of your intuition and your life. They make it safe for you, the high vibration being, to operate through your body and use your spiritual gifts. Historically, psychic gifts have been shrouded in secrecy, only available to mystery school initiates. In this time of shift, turmoil, polarization, and mass awakening, it is necessary to teach them to as many people as possible. You will learn an important lesson that will change your life. It is the secret of enlightenment and how to be conscious as a spirit in a body.

Next, you will be shown how to be in charge of your life, by seating your consciousness in a specific location. By occupying this soul seat, you activate your intuition and can easily handle any information you receive. Once you have this under your belt, I'll explain how to work with energy. You'll discover how to create thought forms. You can use clairvoyance and your ability to manipulate energy to change your reality by letting go of what you don't want and creating what you do.

You can't align to your unique life purpose unless you are oriented to the planet. You will awaken to planet Earth by consciously running Earth energy through your body. This can help you release limits, relieve stress, and clear unwanted energy. You also can't align to your purpose without being oriented to the rest of the cosmos and source energy. You are a multidimensional eternal being. Other aspects of your consciousness are creating in other realities. By consciously running cosmic energy, you balance with cosmic consciousness.

In the final chapter, we bring everything presented in the book together. You will be mentored through exercises to help you identify your Intuition Blueprint and validate how it supports your life purpose. You will be shown how to use meditation to heal your life, clear your limits, and activate your intuition. You will see more clearly and have your own unique spiritual perspective. You will have the tools to transition from where you are now to where you want to be. If you follow these exercises, you will be well on the path to using your intuition as a practical everyday tool that supports all aspects of your life.

To explain your energy system and intuition, I have sliced the information into sections. In reality, however, your chakras and spiritual communication function as an integrated whole.

The first tenet of spiritual growth is to "know yourself." I hope this book will help you know yourself as spirit, and your personal path and purpose more deeply than ever before. Self-awareness and self-healing are the foundation of spiritual growth. If you develop your understanding of your energy system, you can see yourself and heal yourself. Then you can be in a position to give to others if you wish.

As a spark of divine consciousness, you are limitless, there isn't anything you cannot know or create. You are source energy. You are a vibrational being. Your desires fuel your expansion in this reality and many others. Intuition is how you communicate as spirit. You have created a body to experience physical reality. This body is powerful. It has an intellect, emotions, and sex drive. You must be in charge to live a consciously created and intuitively guided life. Most humans have forgotten they are spirit. They focus solely on their physical nature. They use their body aspects, but not their spiritual gifts. This excludes them from expressing their full potential and creativity.

Learning to meditate and develop your ability to communicate as spirit will bridge this gap as it helps you connect body and spirit.

Everyone has intuition. This book will help you tap into yours more than ever before. Intuition can guide your life and answer your questions. It will help you know yourself, know what you want, as well as how to create it.

The Intuition Journey

Throughout this book, there are many stories of individuals and their personal intuition journey. They are meant to inspire and encourage you. These people have overcome many challenges, opened their abilities, and used them to enhance their lives. If they can do it, so can you. As well as sharing these stories, I thought it helpful to share some personal experiences, so that you get to know me, and because I also had challenges. We are all mirrors for one another and can learn from each other's experiences.

I have always loved my intuition, although that was not always the label I used to describe my ability to interact with energy and communicate with spirit. To me, the sky swims with energy and the air is alive with fast-moving particles of light. As a young child, I remember asking my mother, as she tucked me up in bed, if she could see the pretty lights. She said she could not. So I tried to make myself see the same as others. I oriented myself to being in the world, and to seeing with my physical eyes instead of my spiritual eye. I worked hard and was top of the class. This opened possibilities in one way, but it closed them down in another.

I grew up in the United Kingdom in a culture where the intellect was placed on a pedestal. I did a great job of fitting in. I was an environmental microbiologist who searched bio-diverse regions of the planet for natural products to be used as medicines. Like a modern shaman, I believed nature's treasures had the capacity to help and heal. I studied at university for eight years, received a PhD and the best training in experimental design, critical thinking, and the systematic study of the behavior of the natural world.

During the years I was a scientist, I kept a dream diary. My nightly adventures intrigued me, as my dream reality behaved in opposition to the known laws of physical reality. Plenty of scientists have offered theories to explain dreams. But what fascinated me were my direct experiences, which were not being adequately explained, including premonitions of my personal life and world events, meeting people in dreams first before meeting them in my daily life, and past-life scenarios where I recognized friends although they had different bodies.

As well as having a doctorate and career in the life science industry, I followed my passion for developing and using my intuition to guide my life and help others. By the time I moved to Canada, I was already committed to my spiritual growth. Alone in my new country, I searched for like-minded people. I found an organization that offered advanced training in healing and intuition. As a result, my spiritual evolvement accelerated. I spent six years in intense training and have practiced professionally since 2005. I delved deeply into my beliefs and stored pain, freed myself from self-limiting concepts, and let go of external programming. I am a certified intuitive counselor, energy healer, and meditation teacher.

Because my psychic awareness developed at the same time my business career took off, I ended up leading a double life for many years. I once admitted to teaching meditation at a business negotiation lunch. The lady who had asked about my hobbies was perplexed and said, "Is that when hippies do a sit-in on the floor with their legs crossed, chanting?" I thought then that it was best if I kept that side of myself under wraps. I also thought that to be completely accepted by my psychic friends, I had to reject my education, my job, and my past to meld with their expectations of who could be intuitive. I realize now that is far from true, yet I rejected that side of me for a while.

Because of my personal life journey, I am able to bridge the gap between the intellectual and intuitive realms. I am not the stereotype of a scientist, businesswoman, or intuitive—I am me! These days, I mentor individuals in both realms. I help them clarify their direction, transform themselves, and live a more fulfilling life. One of my goals for this book is to break down barriers. Being intuitive is still taboo, and my vision is for it to be accepted as an everyday part of life. Science and spirituality are coming together more than ever before. Yet intuitive practices are not always grounded in this reality, and intellectuals still try to grasp intuition through logic. This book will help you integrate the polarities of intellect and intuition, so you can be sensitive among the intellectuals, grounded among the intuitive people, and authentic with both.

If you were attracted to this book, you might recognize yourself in my story of being pulled in two directions. This book was written for you if you are seeking a higher purpose for your life, are ready to explore your inner world, wish to understand your intuitive experiences, and wish to develop your intuition. It isn't for you if you want to read a thesis on intuition, but if you release doubt and open up to new realizations, you can step into your own direct experiences. Suffice it to say science is catching up. There are peer-reviewed papers with supporting evidence, including studies on intuition in military defense, sports coaching, emergency medicine, physics, and biology. If you want scientific evidence, you can find it in other books.[1] I can guide you in your inner work and show you how to heal yourself. Let go of your illusions, expectations, and limits. Dig deeper, look under rocks, be your authentic self, be intuitive, and be self-aware.

If you read this book and stay committed to your growth, you will propel yourself on an accelerated journey of awakening. This book is for you if you want to learn to receive higher guidance, trust your intuition, release doubt, clear your blocks, and act on your intuition. You have selected the right book if you believe in your intuition, want to learn your intuition style, and wish to develop it further. You are on the right journey if you have had unexplained experiences, feel blocked in accessing your intuition, and wish to know why; or if you have trouble trusting or acting on your intuitive messages and want to overcome your doubt and uncertainty.

If you are wondering whether you are ready to take this step, here are a few things to consider:

- Are you happy with everything in your life or do you wish you could change some things?
- Do you have a strong desire to heal yourself, and can you commit to doing everything it takes to be transformed?
- Is something missing that you know should be there?

---

1. Gober, Mark. *An End to Upside Down Thinking: Dispelling the Myth That the Brain Produces Consciousness, and the Implications for Everyday Life.* Cardiff-By-the-Sea: Waterside Press, 2018.

The path of the intuitive is a personal journey that can take time. You can truly shift your reality when you are committed to your personal growth. Developing my intuition changed my life completely in powerful ways. I hope this book inspires you to reclaim and use your gifts.

Part One
INTUITION AND YOUR ENERGY

Chapter I
YOUR INTUITION

At birth, spiritual abilities are active in all of us, but for many people they are turned down over time. This happens as you orient to the physical world, because you must learn to operate your body and its senses for feedback about physical reality. The extent of intuitive shutdown depends on culture and upbringing. If the intuitive senses are ignored or discouraged, they become inactive. Some people are so focused on material existence, they stop experiencing intuition completely. Given that you are reading this book, you are likely not one of those people; though perhaps you sense your intuition could be stronger and want to reclaim your inner guidance system. Luckily, you can remember and fully reactivate your abilities.

The association of the third eye with spiritual vision and the crown chakra as a gateway to higher consciousness are well known. Yet there are other energy centers that play a role in spiritual communication. There are seven major chakras that channel intuitive abilities and information that can guide your life journey. *Intuition Blueprint* is a term I coined to describe the road map of your unique spiritual abilities. You are meant to be conscious as a spirit in your body and use these psychic gifts to guide your life. As you read this book, you will go through a process to discover yours. It is a framework to help describe your unique guidance system

Knowing your Intuition Blueprint provides insight into how you wish to use your gifts to support your life purpose. It sheds light on how you are or are not using them. Most teachers say the first step in spiritual evolvement is self-knowledge. Accessing your Intuition Blueprint opens the door to self-knowledge so you can navigate your life. Your Intuition Blueprint helps clarify your life goals as well as explain why you might be self-sabotaging. It informs you about your unique intuition style and how you can use it to create a fulfilling life that aligns with your greatest good. The information in the Intuition Blueprint stimulates your awareness and sows seeds of change deep within your consciousness. If you understand you are spirit, came here for a reason, and have an amazing internal support system to help you achieve your desires, then you can address everything that is getting in your way of reaching your desired potential.

Your Potential as an Awakened Human

Before you were born, you selected which spiritual powers you would tap into and develop to achieve your life goals. This profile is unique to you and supports you throughout this incarnation. Your Intuition Blueprint tells you which spiritual abilities you are focusing on in this lifetime and why. Its configuration at birth tells you how you are meant to play your instrument for beautiful music in the symphony of souls. Your Intuition Blueprint today helps you see if you are aligned with your Trusted Source and using your gifts to your full potential or if you are ignoring them. This knowledge helps you clear blocks and reclaim your gifts.

You will be surprised at how quickly you can unblock your intuition and use it to improve your everyday life. No matter what your current financial, relationship, or career situation, access to intuition can improve your life circumstances and show you how you can be of service in the world. You may be amazed at how many different ways there are for receiving intuitive information. While you have five physical senses, there are many more intuitive senses. Table 1 introduces you to the relationship between the chakras and psychic abilities. We will discuss each of them in detail in Part Two, where I hope you will begin to remember your unique intuitive abilities as well as start to use them to access guidance from your Trusted Source.

Chakra	Ability	Explanation
First (Root)	Survival	Programming to keep your body alive
Second (Sacral)	Clairsentience	Feeling emotions of self and others
Third (Solar Plexus)	Energy Distribution	Supplies vital energy through the body
	Astral Experience	Out-of-body dream experiences
	Astral Memory	Recollection of the dream state
Fourth (Heart)	Affinity	Attractive force drawing you to others and your passion
	Oneness	Connecting with all consciousness
Fifth (Throat)	Inner Voice	How you talk to your body personality
	Clairaudience	Hearing beings without bodies
	Broadband Telepathy	Nonverbal communication to groups
	Narrow Band Telepathy	Nonverbal communication to one or two others
	Pragmatic Intuition	Dealing with practical affairs
Sixth (Brow/ Third Eye)	Clairvoyance	Seeing spiritual phenomena clearly
	Abstract Intuition	Relating to abstract information
Seventh (Crown)	Trance Mediumship	Channeling spirit—yours or others
	Claircognizance/ Knowingness	Being still and knowing things
Sixth, Seventh	Precognition	Knowing the future

Chakra	Ability	Explanation
Hands, 6, 7	Psychometry	Telling things such as the past of an object by touch
Hands, 6, 7, 1	Healing	Healing yourself and other people
Hands, 6, 7, 1	Telekinesis	Altering the molecular state of an object with your will
Hands	Manifestation	Manifesting your inner creativity outwardly
Feet	Earth Energy	Drawing in energy from Earth

Table 1: Summary of Intuitive Abilities

Intuition and Your Akashic Record

You are an infinite being of ever-expanding wisdom and creative expression. You create in many realities, including Earth. The record of your imprint on the fabric of time and space is known as your Akashic Record. Everything about you, all you have done, thought, and felt in all your lives and other experiences of consciousness are recorded in your Akashic Record. Your Intuition Blueprint is the part of this record that relates to your spiritual abilities and how you use them in this life.

You are infinite consciousness. You could not fit the full expression of who you are into one body or lifetime. Nor would it make sense to do so. You create each life as a pocket of experience. You stay connected to the greater pool of knowledge through your intuition. Your intuition provides that connection to your full Akashic Record and higher guidance. It can also connect you to other parts of yourself, including past lives and higher levels of consciousness. It allows you to communicate with your soul about your life plan.

An analogy for this is to think about how DNA works. DNA is the blueprint of life. That blueprint is translated and expressed to create the biochemistry and physical structures of your body. If your soul is your DNA, then your Intuition Blueprint is the expression of that DNA through your life experience.

Awakening Your Intuition

Knowing you are spirit is the first step in your awakening. Accepting you have a wider range of sensory apparatus than your body is not so strange once you make that leap. To use your abilities to their potential, you must realize what caused you to turn away from them. You must want to see your life clearly, be willing to let go of the past, and accept major shifts in your thoughts, beliefs, behavior, and circumstances.

Owning and activating your spiritual system is like doing a home renovation. You need to examine the underlying structures that hold up the house and check that they are sound. If they are not, replace them with new ones. Once you check the foundations and ensure the structure is sound you can begin, taking care to clean the mess that gets stirred up. As you clean, you may look in places you haven't been in years and find old things you had forgotten. What emerges from the rubble may horrify or delight you. The old décor may have been influenced by someone else's taste. Maybe your old style was done to make someone else happy; live up to cultural, religious, or familial expectations; or fit better into the neighborhood.

In this analogy, the house represents your life. Foundations and structures are your beliefs. The décor is programming on how to behave. Now is the ideal time to decorate in your unique style and make a comfortable home for you to inhabit. Your chakras are like the vents that allow fresh air inside. If they are clogged with the debris of pain and invalidation, you will never breathe the clean air of your higher wisdom. Cleansing the chakras is necessary for owning your intuitive abilities. Meditation is the most powerful way I know to cleanse your chakra system and awaken your intuitive gifts.

Validating Your Intuition

The best way to validate your intuition is to experience it. It isn't something that can be studied and understood academically as it operates beyond the body and intellect. People fear what they can't understand. In our time period, intuitive people have been labeled as misguided crackpots. Some religious people say it is evil, and intellectuals label it as unscientific.

While admitting you follow your intuition can get you into trouble, usually it doesn't advance beyond ridicule. However, in the past, it could get you killed. Joan of Arc was a rural peasant who heard voices that told her about her destiny as the leader of an army that would reclaim Orleans from the English. The voices told her where to find a sword buried in a church and instructed her to use it. Unfortunately, Joan was convicted of witchcraft and burned at the stake in 1431. Five hundred years later, she was declared a saint.

Throughout history, there are many other similar examples, including the healers and herbalists who were tried and executed as witches and the seers who were punished for seeing what others didn't want known. Luckily things are changing. Before the turn of the century, meditation was considered out of the ordinary and now it is mainstream. It has been introduced to schools and the workplace. Our scientists and business schools have studied it and have learned to see its value.

Psychologists have also turned their attention to intuition. They want to train people in quick decision making in situations where there is no time for analytical reasoning. Military strategists want to understand intuition to help soldiers and medics make fast decisions in the theatre of war. In fact, the U.S. Navy has funded research to enhance intuitive decision making.[2] Family physicians, emergency room doctors, and nurses are also being studied to understand how they use intuition and reason in life-and-death situations.[3,4] In a study performed by the Smith School of Business, 78 percent of business leaders admitted using intuition when they don't have time to weigh up the pros and cons.[5]

Most people believe in intuition when it is accessed in the dream state. This is an accepted "mystery" because nearly all of us have direct experience of dreaming. Indeed, studies have shown that most people have had a

2. Squire, Peter, et al. Enhancing Intuitive Decision Making Through Implicit Learning. *Interservice/Industry Training, Simulation, and Education Conference* (I/ITSEC), 2014.

3. Woolley, Amanda, et al. Clinical intuition in family medicine: more than first impressions. *Annals of Family Medicine.* 11. 1 (Jan 2013): 60-6.

4. Lyneham J, et al. Explicating Benner's concept of expert practice: intuition in emergency nursing. *Journal of Advanced Nursing.* 64. 4 (Nov. 2008): 380-7.

5. The Smith School of Business. Executive Survey. Smith School of Business. www.smith. queensu.ca Accessed April 20, 2019. https://smith.queensu.ca/news_blog/2016/2016-05-10_Data_Analytics_Survey.php

precognitive dream.[6] Yet, few are able to consistently access intuition from waking consciousness, nor believe this possible. So intuition usually happens during sleep or when the desire to know is strong. For instance, it has been demonstrated that 70 percent of pregnant women can predict their baby's sex.[7]

The above studies are a great validation for intuition, especially for those who need factual evidence and rational explanations. However, an intellectual approach can muddy the waters and result in confusion if it reduces intuition to mechanistic explanations and ignores the spiritual aspect.

Current scientific theories on "intuitive intelligence" have categorized three types of intuition. First is implicit learning, where the brain uses pattern matching to connect the dots between new problems and forgotten knowledge acquired in the past. Second is energetic sensitivity when the nervous system detects and responds to electromagnetic fields, which explains the sense of being stared at. Third is nonlocal intuition, which is the capacity to receive and process information about nonlocal events, thought to be due to the interconnectedness of everything in the universe.

Parapsychologists studying extrasensory perception (ESP) have historically categorized the psychic senses into four main types of PSI phenomena: telepathy, precognition, clairvoyance, and psychokinesis. They test for it in controlled experiments using methods such as Zener cards, where the subject must predict which of five shapes will be the next card in the deck to be upturned. Parapsychology also studies near-death experiences, synchronicity, reincarnation, apparitional experiences, and other paranormal claims. If you wish to know more about the scientific studies on psychic abilities, *An End to Upside Down Thinking: Dispelling the Myth That the Brain Produces Consciousness, and the Implications for Everyday Life,* by Mark Gober, describes hundreds of them.[8]

6. Wilson, Ian A. Theory of Precognitive Dreams. www.academia.edu Accessed April 20, 2019. https://www.academia.edu/8089263/Theory_of_Precognitive_Dreams

7. Shamas, Victor. The Intuition Pregnancy Study 1998. www.victorshamas.com Accessed April 20th 2019. https://www.victorshamas.com/intuition-study.html

8. Gober. *An End to Upside Down Thinking.*

Demystifying Your Intuition

I personally believe there are twenty-two different aspects that make up your unique Intuition Blueprint. Some of these psychic abilities are studied by mainstream science and some of them are not. The Intuition Blueprint system is based on the chakras and the different ways of communicating that are channeled through them. I developed this system from my knowledge and lineage in practicing the ancient mystery teachings.

Most, if not all, of the world's ancient religions have taught meditation as a path to enlightenment and recognize psychic abilities as a consequence of such practices. Such teachings are present in Daoist alchemical practices; Hinduism, where they are called Siddhis; and Buddhism, where they are known as iddhis. There is a general consensus about what is possible for the spiritual master. Traditionally, few individuals receive the teachings. Their teachers often stress the goal is enlightenment and not the abilities themselves.

In Hinduism, some psychic abilities, including claircognizance, precognition, and telepathy, are said to be more common and accessible. Other common abilities are mastering opposites by withstanding hot and cold; stopping the effects of water, fire, and poison; and being unable to be manipulated by others. Over the natural course of meditation practice, additional Siddhis are said to develop. These are clairaudience, clairvoyance, manifestation, teleportation, out-of-body experience, astral travel, shape-shifting, entering other people's bodies, inter-dimensional awareness, and observing non-physical beings. The practitioner doesn't have thirst, hunger, or other physical appetites, and can choose when they die. Finally, the Siddhis[9] attained by advanced practitioners include the ability to do anything and fulfill any desire. This includes becoming smaller than a subatomic particle, being as large as the universe, going inside and through objects, being any frequency of light, and traveling in the light body. It also includes advanced manifestation such as creating objects out of thin air, walking on fire or water, and controlling the actions of other beings.

9. Sri Swami Satchidananda. *The Yoga Sutras of Patanjali*. Buckingham: Integral Yoga Publications, 2012.

It may sound like science fiction, but through direct knowledge and meditation practice, these abilities are possible. It can take lifetimes to become a master who manipulates matter, but psychic communication as presented in this book is possible for you now. I have not met anyone who wanted to unlock these abilities and came to me for guidance who couldn't access at least one of the clair-abilities. The Intuition Blueprint is based on the ancient mystery teachings. These include the origins mentioned above but were also known in ancient Egypt, by the Essenes and other groups, and in Atlantis and Lemuria—all of which are part of my multidimensional lineage for knowing and teaching this information. Like me, you have had other lives where you practiced spiritual abilities. Your intuition can help you discover this if you wish.

My goal in writing this book is to make psychic abilities understandable and accessible in a practical way at a time when this information is to be made available to all rather than the few. We have reached a tipping point on this planet, where we have the potential to step into a New Earth[10] and become a new version of the human species.[11] People are awakening en masse because of the increased vibration in our world. I offer the information in this book as a support choice during this time to help you access your higher guidance in whatever form it takes for you, so you can live your highest potential and stay true to your purpose and your part in this great adventure.

Intuition and Life Purpose

Your unique profile of intuitive abilities and your life purpose fit together like a hand in a glove. Here are some real-life examples of people whose intuition helped them consciously live their life purpose. Reading them might help inspire you to see how your intuition and purpose are connected.

Faye Envisions a Better Future

Faye's Intuition Blueprint indicated her purpose related to shifting collective consciousness by being a visionary futurist. She wanted to create games that

10. Tolle, Eckhart. *A New Earth: Awakening to Your Life's Purpose*. New York: Penguin Books, 2008.
11. Walsch, Neale Donald. *Conversations with God, Book 4: Awaken the Species*. Faber: Rainbow Ridge Books, 2017.

helped people enter states of greater joy and happiness. Even though she was a student, she already had a great business idea. Her chart showed a lot of activity in the sixth chakra, in abstract intuition and clairvoyance, as well as precognition, healing, and manifestation. She used her abilities to envision and create inventions that could help uplift humanity.

Callan Exposes Government Secrets

My friend Callan's purpose was focused on bringing attention to global injustice. He used to work in defense at a classified facility where he was exposed to secret military research. Once he left this career, he exposed news stories of governments and corporations lying to people. His chart showed a focus on communication, healing, oneness, and affinity. His life path took him on a journey from working in secrecy to unmasking hidden truths to the masses.

Dawna Speaks Up for Change

Dawna Jones believes her purpose is to influence how businesses make decisions by helping them shift from a profit-based to a prosperity model, and by revitalizing the environment and those impacted by the business and its employees. Her Intuition Blueprint showed emphasis on the fourth and fifth chakras. Her heart's passion guided her to rise above adversity to be a speaker who connects people through leadership and spirit. Her Earth energy was also a focus as she is an environmental steward working to make a beneficial impact on the environment and society.

Jerry Wants to Build Community

Jerry had given up his job and sold his possessions. His greatest desire was to create an intentional community with other like-minded individuals. He had been wandering the Earth for eighteen months searching for his tribe. His Intuition Blueprint showed a focus on his heart chakra because he was expanding his affinity for the planet and helping to create a place of belonging for like-minded people. His clairvoyance helped him focus on his vision and his inner knowing to have faith that he knew how to make his dream a reality.

Briana Nurtures Body and Soul

Briana came here to nourish the soul. She started as a chef and expanded to develop a school dedicated to inner health. She had a high level of clairsentience as it was important for her to listen to the body's signals and help keep it healthy. She also had well-developed communication and visionary aspects and a strong ability to manifest, all of which helped her create her health-focused businesses.

Amy Solves Crimes Intuitively

Amy's reading showed she was focused on using clairvoyance, psychometry, and clairsentience. Amy, a detective, was skilled at her job and devoted to it. She used her abilities to solve crimes, even though she had not been calling it intuition. When attending a crime scene, Amy reconstructed what had happened by feeling the situation in action as if she was there while the crime was taking place. Like many people, Amy had challenges separating her energy from others until she learned to clear her energy field and discern the energy from victims and perpetrators.

Chapter 2
YOUR LIFE PURPOSE

Over the last few years, I have been blessed to be the host of a local radio show focused on personal development.[12] In that time, nearly a thousand listeners have contacted me with their life questions. Nearly half asked, "What is my purpose?" Being curious, I started asking the crowds who came to my workshops two questions: "Who believes they have a life purpose?" and "Who knows what their purpose is?"

Without exception, everyone believed they had a purpose yet only a small fraction knew what it was. After reviewing the problems my clients asked me about, I realized they also struggle to identify their purpose. More than anything, people want to develop their potential, overcome their blocks, and make a difference in the world. It therefore astounds me that so many feel lost, especially when I know how you can understand your life and find your unique purpose. The key is the relationship between your intuition and chakras, which is your internal guidance system for life. I am encouraged that so many bright, powerful individuals want to make a difference. If each is helped to shed their limits and freely express their potential, our world can be different.

Most people believe they have a higher purpose, but they have no idea what it is. As a consequence, life does not feel focused, and they struggle to find meaning. Some have a vague notion but are not deeply in touch with their purpose. Even those who know their purpose admit they have not

---

12. *Unlocking Your Truth with Dr. Lesley* past episodes: https://drlesleyphillips.com/category/podcast

always known it, and that they still experience times of uncertainty. We have all spent sleepless nights questioning our life choices. We are not always consciously creating our lives in alignment with our purpose, even if we do know what it is.

My purpose is to be an intuitive messenger and teacher. I express this in my work as a writer, radio host, and mentor. In my awakening journey, I spent years as a scientist and businesswoman. On the surface my life was fabulous. I had a great job that paid well and allowed me to travel the world. Playing the role of the person I thought I was meant to be was not fulfilling, however. I didn't believe the real me was good enough so I covered her with a blanket of other people's expectations. My pain caused me to seek answers. I wanted greater meaning to my life. My search led me to wonderful people, places, and experiences, and I learned everything I needed to create the life I desired.

I discovered I came here with an instruction manual and toolkit for my life. My toolkit contains a global positioning device that tells me where I am right now and a navigation system that gives clear directions. I also have an abundance of talents that are precisely what I need to support my journey.

You also have an instruction manual and toolbox that contain exactly what you need for your life plan. The positioning device is your energy field. It contains complete information about your life, and how you are living. It locates you in the present moment, has a record of where you were, and shows you where you are headed.

The chakras provide the navigation. They form your energy field, process your life experiences, and provide you with a direct line to your higher guidance. They are conduits for intuition to flow from your higher consciousness to your temporal self. While your intuition provides guidance, the different forms of intuition are the talents that make up your Intuition Blueprint. If you unlock these gifts, you can chart your direction, steer your course effectively, champion your growth, and live according to your purpose.

You have several life purposes: enlightenment, your unique contribution, and the eternal pursuit of expansion.

Understanding Enlightenment

You are not simply your physical body, you are spirit. In fact, you are a multidimensional eternal being of love and light. Your body is a vehicle you created to have focused experiences in physical reality, which are meant to expand your consciousness. To do that, you need to occupy your body and take charge of it, so you can consciously create your experiences through it. When you occupy your body, you fill it with your light. In other words, you enlighten it.

Enlightenment is also about becoming lighter. It is about you raising the vibration of your body, so it can comfortably be occupied by your consciousness, and so you can wake up inside yourself and be consciously aware. This is a common purpose of all of humanity.

Master teachers such as Jesus, Buddha, and Mohammed showed us how to do this through their life stories. They were way-showers, who wanted to help us all lighten up and realize our own mastery. They were all masters of balance and duality, which is why they were able to perform miracles and demonstrate highly advanced abilities such as changing water into wine, materializing loaves and fishes, parting the Red Sea, and walking on water. They were psychics and energy healers and used their abilities to help them fulfill their purpose on Earth. They followed their higher guidance, communicated as spirit, and healed themselves and others. Like these teachers, everyone is unique and has a matchless contribution they can make to this world.

Your Unique Contribution

Imagine humanity as a great symphony; each individual being a finely tuned instrument, with a unique note to play in a magnificent opus. To play your unique note, you must understand how your instrument works. You must discover the correct keys, strings, or finger holds that will produce the perfect pitch and tone. As in an orchestra, the tuba can't play the part that was written for the violin. The tuba can only do justice to the part that was written for the tuba.

Every human is a unique musical instrument. When correctly tuned, you are capable of playing beautiful music, written exclusively for you. This music is your life purpose. No one else can play your note. Only you can. If you do not play it, the symphony will lose harmony. You will do yourself and fellow musicians a great disservice. This is why it makes no sense to compare yourself to, or try to emulate, another. If you play someone else's note, then no one is playing yours. There will be a gap in the symphony and the other musicians may feel unworthy, as someone else is playing their part.

As a soul, you have many capabilities—so many you cannot fit them into one body. You decide before birth what you will focus on. You set parameters such as when, where, and to whom you will be born. You decide what you wish to experience, and how you want to grow. You select a physical body that can support it. You also determine which of your skills, wisdom, and spiritual abilities you will emphasize to support your goals.

Here's a great analogy. David has the potential to be a physics professor, carpenter, gardener, chef, and athlete. He has spent many jobs (lifetimes) honing his skills in each of these areas. For his next job (life) he has decided that he wants to expand his skills as a carpenter. He determines he must take his saw, adze, and sandpaper. He carefully picks them out and places them in his tool belt. David does not need his rake, calculator, or his pots and pans so he puts them aside for another time, especially as his tool belt only has the space for a certain number of tools. He also agrees to work with a joiner, painter, and plasterer (soul group members) whose goals align with his. David also takes into account the locale where he will work (be born). They may have different customs and use slightly different tools in one country than another, or at one time versus another (on the planet), depending on the larger job at hand.

Your Intuition Blueprint is just like this. You, the eternal being, have many aspects—so many that you could not fit them all into one lifetime. You choose what is most relevant and helpful given what you plan to focus on.

Life Purpose, Personal Goals, and Free Will

There is a difference between life purpose and life goals. You may believe your purpose is to be a foreign ambassador. This is a goal rather than your purpose, though your attraction to this role may be because your purpose is exploring peace within yourself and others. As a stay-at-home mum, you may be frustrated, believing that looking after demanding kids keeps you from your purpose as a university professor. Let's say your purpose is really to learn to own your personal space and express your authentic voice. Both roles are opportunities to explore this; you can experience your purpose in different ways. Even when you think you are not on your path, you are always having an experience that serves your purpose to expand.

You are consciousness projected into the matrix of time and space on Earth. Here you experience separation and polarity. You have free will and can make choices about how you live. Your choices help you navigate physical reality. They may be conscious or unconscious, but either way, they take you up to peaks, and down to valleys of your life path. You get to explore the landscape of your uniqueness along the way.

As spirit, there is oneness, eternity, and inter-connectedness. Many of us spend our whole life yearning for the love and peace we know exists but which seems elusive. We long to return to our source. Life on this planet is a series of ups and downs for everyone, and the soul delights in new experiences. From a spiritual perspective, there are no good or bad life events. Only experiences to play out for the purpose of expansion. While you might strive for a life with more ups than downs, both are grist for the mill of your expansion.

If you believe there is a way to get your life just right, think again; there is no right and wrong. Instead, there is you in the eternal moment of now, making choices and experiencing results. If you judge your choices when you don't like the outcome, you remain stuck. Instead, if you realize you just experienced something that you do not prefer, you can move on. If you blame others for the unfortunate circumstances of your life, you are giving your power away. When you take responsibility, you take charge and steer the boat in a different direction. All experiences are equally valid and fuel your expansion. No matter what choices you do or do not make, or how you live out your life, you will fulfill your purpose to expand in consciousness. You will have new experiences never had by anyone before, and in doing so add to the expansion of all consciousness. You will change and you will grow. If you do it consciously rather than unconsciously, you may find you manifest a more joyful life.

Manifestation and the Law of Attraction

How you grow is down to you. The circumstances you attract into your life hinge on the energy you put out, including your thoughts, beliefs, actions, and general energy vibration. The basic principle is that our universe works on attraction and combines energies that are a vibrational match. If you can manage your vibration, you can guide your reality. According to the universal laws of our reality:

- You create your reality through your beliefs.
- Like attracts like so you get what you are.
- Everything in your reality was put in it by you.
- Everyone in your reality shows you your reflection
- You are unique and yet you are a mirror for others.

What this means in terms of your life creations is you can create a pleasant or unpleasant journey depending on your beliefs. You can be at peace or at war within yourself. If you choose to awaken your intuitive senses, you will be able to observe how your life creations are linked to your beliefs more easily. If you learn how to consciously manage your energy, you will be able to change your limiting ideas into more supportive ones.

Your growth experiences are reflected in the energy field that surrounds your body. Everything about you, including your spiritual unfolding, unique purpose, and life goals can be observed through your intuitive senses. This book shows you how to create a pleasant journey by managing your energy, healing yourself, and accessing your higher guidance for what you wish to create and what choices you will make.

While the specific techniques for energy management appear in Part Three, certain principles underpin the ability to consciously attract your preferred life experiences. Here, then, are seven basic steps for creating your reality in accordance with the law of attraction:

1. **Know what you want.** You must decide what you want to use the law of attraction for. Some people are poor creators because they don't know what they want. This often happens to those who devote their

energy to taking care of others. When you focus on pleasing others or putting their needs first, you can become so out of balance it doesn't even occur to you that you actually have needs.

2. **Ask for it to be created.** Once you know what you want, it's important to prioritize it and ask for it. There are various techniques you can use for this, such as using your imagination to visualize it, writing it down, or creating a vision board to solidify your intentions. Whatever technique you use, be as detailed as possible. At the same time, allow some leeway for the unexpected. We can be limited in our thinking about what is possible.

3. **Believe you can have it.** Sometimes people are good at following techniques, but they fall down when it actually comes to believing they can create what they want. You have to eliminate all doubt or contrary beliefs. Otherwise, your creation will not manifest, or at the very least will take a long time to come into being. If you blame others when your life doesn't go how you'd like, you give your power away, you don't believe in yourself.

4. **Be the vibration of it.** The more you can be the vibration of what you are asking for the more likely it is to appear in your reality. If you focus on wanting something in the future because you do not have it now, you will perpetuate that situation. However, if you act as though you already have what you want and are enjoying it, the easier it will slip into your reality experience.

5. **Recognize it when it arrives.** There is a well-known story about a man trapped on his roof in a flood, expecting God to rescue him. When a neighbor rows past and offers him a ride and a rescue helicopter drops him a rope, he says, "No, thank you; I am waiting for God to save me." The moral of the story is he didn't recognize his wish was answered because it didn't come in the form he expected. If you asked for a tall dark handsome man, don't turn down the redhead. Give him a chance; he might be the closest match to what you asked for.

6. **Receive it, allow it, and have it.** Being able to receive can be another barrier for some people. They can be fantastic at manifesting, but

they are unable to receive what they have created because they do not believe they deserve it. They do not let themselves have and enjoy their creations, so the creations slip through their fingers like sand. Let go of invalidation and unworthiness so you can feel good about having what you want.

7. **Don't resist or control your creations.** When we forget we are creating our life, whether we like what shows up in it or not, we can get into resistance with what is. So long as we resist, what we resist persists. It is necessary to accept your life as it is right now before you can change it into something you would prefer. Likewise, do not try to control the creation process, but allow the universal principle to do its job. Your job is to ask and the universe will respond. If you attempt to control it, you will limit what is created because you cannot conceive of all the ways your creation can come to you.

The law of attraction goes by many names, including the Law of Abundance, Karma, and Cause and Effect. They are all based on the same information. I also like to call it the Law of Personal Responsibility and Empowerment. If you create your reality, then you are responsible for your creations. You are also empowered because it means you have the potential to be a conscious creator of that reality. Whatever is in your reality now is an aspect of you being reflected back at you. So pay attention as it is teaching you something about yourself. It is telling you what is in your energy field.

Life Purpose and Passion

Your purpose exists on many levels, from enlightenment to purpose in each moment. Your intuition can help you connect with the cosmos and your multidimensional nature; talk to your personal God and receive divine guidance as well as be practical here and now. Your unique life purpose can manifest differently at different stages of life and can change over time. Most people go through different stages of experiencing their purpose. A parent's main purpose could be child-rearing until the kids grow up, then they switch to other creative projects. Someone with a desire to be a healer may go through a period of intense self-healing before helping others. You might have a desire to learn something and, if you complete this purpose before your life ends, your circumstances could change significantly as you choose and live out a new purpose.

IDENTIFYING YOUR LIFE PASSIONS EXERCISE

Clues to your present purpose for this lifetime lie in what you feel passionate about. In this exercise, you will make a list of everything you love now, as well as a historical list of what you loved through different stages of your life. Then you will review what you wrote for overarching themes.

1. Make a list of everything you feel passionate about. Note for each one if it is for sheer joy or because you wish to create or change it. Review your notes and identify clues to your life purpose.

2. Make another list of your childhood dreams and creative desires. Note which ones came true and validate your ability to follow your passion and purpose. For those that didn't happen yet, cross out the ones that don't apply to you now. Review the remainder and ask why they didn't come true. Notice if there are any common themes that stand out.

3. Keep these notes handy as you will need them in Part Three.

Chapter 3
YOUR ENERGY FIELD

We are now embarking on a journey through your spiritual system. Starting here, I will introduce you to the human energy field, which is your personal creative universe and is also known as the aura.

- The aura is an energy bubble surrounding your body.
- It is multidimensional in nature.
- It emanates from your chakras.
- It defines your personal space.
- It is your creative universe.
- You are meant to be the master of this universe.
- You determine what will be created through it.

The aura has been called the "fingerprint of God" because it contains all the information about you. I like to think of it as a global positioning device because by being aware of your aura, you can tell where you are, in a physical, mental, emotional, and spiritual sense. Being able to read the aura has been a powerful tool in my energy practice because it helps me very quickly get to the core of any matter, whether my client is asking about intuition development, life purpose, health, romance, abundance, career, or anything else.

I will start this chapter by sharing my information about the aura, which has been accumulated over many years of experience observing thousands of energy fields. When I first started out, I read my own aura as a daily practice. It helped me get to know myself deeply, validate myself, and see what I wanted to change and heal. I believe everyone can benefit by learning to read their own energy field. This will become possible for you when you develop your intuition.

Characteristics of the Aura

The aura is a vibrational field of energy. It can be observed intuitively as clouds of fast-moving or slow-moving colors. The vibrational field emanates from energy centers called chakras as inter-penetrating layers of energy. These layers relate to the chakras, vibrate at different frequencies, and can be seen separately by an experienced intuitive. Everyone has their own unique energy composition. Each auric layer relates to your specific circumstances. There is no correct color for your aura, nor is there only one color. It is your coat of many colors. The aura is in constant flux. It is always changing depending on your reality and how you process experiences. It is your unique energy signature as you exist right here, right now.

My favorite analogy for teaching about the aura is to reference the cuttlefish in its natural habitat. These marine cephalopods change their patterns and colors when they have different experiences. Patterns of light flutter across the surface of their skin to ward off predators, attract mates, express mood, help blend in with surroundings, and communicate with other cuttlefish. If you haven't seen one, search for a video online and watch it. Even though you can see the cuttlefish with your physical eyes, and you can only see the aura with your inner eye, this analogy can help you get a general idea before you develop your clairvoyance and see it for yourself.

Each auric layer relates to a different aspect of you and your life experiences such as survival, relationships, energy focus, connectedness, communication, clarity, and higher wisdom. All of your thoughts, beliefs, memories, and emotions relating to your life experiences are stored in your aura as structured units of electromagnetic energy. An experienced clairvoyant can read these units, which may look like symbols, images, pictures, and videos. Your aura reflects everything about you. Its energy components and frequencies indicate your present state of being, including whether you are healthy, your emotional state, and the concepts and beliefs you are operating from.

So long as the energy of your aura is moving there is health. If the energy field is bright and clear, there is physical, mental, and emotional well-being. A dark and cloudy aura indicates issues. To my clairvoyant vision, white can sometimes indicate fear; grey, being caught in the past; dark red, anger; and black, emotional pain or even hatred. These lower vibrations can cause a disturbance in your reality on an emotional or mental level. If stored in your system for a long time, they can manifest as physical illness. Disease happens when the flow of energy through your body does not run smoothly. This can be caused by unsupportive beliefs, low vibration emotions, and stored pain. It is possible for you to intuitively communicate with and heal your body at the systems, organ, and cellular level. Developing awareness of your aura allows you to see what you wish to alter. When you understand the true state of your being, you can change anything you need to.

Being Aware of Your Aura

If you have ever had an experience where a stranger was uncomfortably close, or there was an uncomfortable distance between you and another person, then you are already aware of your energy field. To consciously tune in to it, close your eyes, feel it around you, and sense the boundaries of your personal space. A comfortable distance is usually about an arm's length. It could be farther out or in; your space can expand or contract depending on where you are, how you feel, and who you are with. Be still, and with your eyes closed be aware of circumstances where you naturally have your energy field spread out, and when you pull it close in.

When alone or speaking to a group, your personal energy bubble might fill the room. When you drive it may encompass the car, or when you are outdoors it might be expanded to experience the joys of nature. When you are in a busy shopping mall, you may keep your energy close so as not to be overwhelmed. When you enter a crowded elevator or train, you might contract it to avoid the other energy bubbles. We all expand and contract our personal space naturally. Yet the norms in certain groups differ. High population cities and cultures, where people live in close quarters, can result in a narrow personal space bubble.

All things on Earth, including people, animals, and inanimate objects, have an energy field around them. You can use your intuition to sense your creative space and distinguish it from that of another. If you own your personal space and do not allow other people's energy to stay inside your bubble, you will be able to fulfill your higher purpose and share your message. If you do not dilute your energy by invading the space of others, you will have everything you need to shine brightly. If you are invasive to others, or a host to some foreign energy, you will find it more difficult to fulfill your purpose as you won't have access to all your energy and potential.

Ideally, your energy bubble goes all around your body and encases you like an eggshell. It defines the limits of your personal space. Everything inside it is your creative universe. All that is outside it is someone or something else. You are meant to preside over your personal sphere of reality. Other people have their own personal energy bubble to create through. It is imperative for each to be self-contained energetically and to respect the integrity of others. Otherwise, chaos and confusion will reign. Intuition can help you see when you are out of integrity so you can pull your energy back to you and release foreign energy. You can use intuition to communicate with the higher aspects of yourself and line up with your higher purpose.

The Aura and Reality Creation

If you are not new to the spiritual path, you might be aware of "the law of one," meaning that ultimately we are one and all separation is illusion. Though we are all one, we also experience ourselves as individuated consciousness. In the oneness, all our creations exist simultaneously and desire is not separated from the result. Here on Earth we experience the results of creativity reflected back as cause and effect, and through the mirroring of others whom appear separate from us. We purposefully step out of oneness, into the realm of duality, time, space, and separation, so that we can make choices, focus on the results of our actions, and grow by creating change and exploring our preferences. Each human is a fragment of divine consciousness with its own reality creation field. To fully engage in the physical reality game and see our creations in action, we need to each own our individual energy field.

You create your reality through the energy that you are. This happens unconsciously when you are not self-aware, but can happen consciously when you develop your intuition and heal yourself through meditation. Everything inside your aura is meant to be you. When you own this space, you create your reality through your own energy and intentions. If you don't own it, you will create through other energies present. The other energies in your aura may include the energy of others, and programming from cultural influences. This foreign energy can cause you to lose touch with your own beliefs, and live according to someone else's. If you have stored pain, you will look out through pain, and this is what others will see when looking at you. If you are full of hate, fear, jealousy, or other low vibrations, they will color your reality. Because you exist within your own energy field, the world sees you through this veil of energy. You also see the world through this filter.

Learning to read your aura using your intuition is the ultimate in self-awareness. Reading your energy field is like reading the book of you. Healing your aura is like editing and writing the book of you. By being conscious of its contents, you can see what is, release what you don't want, and create what you do.

Your Intuition and Your Aura

In a world where everyone is in tune with their intuition, the aura is the ultimate communication device. It would not be possible to be in denial or lie, because everyone would see you exactly as you are in any given moment. Our civilization would be different if we operated from our intuition. We would not live in fear and denial. Instead, we would see and appreciate each person for their unique beauty and truth. Most people only use a fraction of their intuition so the limits of the intellect and the facades of the ego prevail. This has led to a false projected reality and masking deeper insights about who we are and what we are doing as a species.

The aura is the window to your soul. It is also the window you perceive reality through. If you own it, then your window is clean and you can perceive reality clearly. If it is full of unsupportive energies, then your window is dirty and your view is blocked. If you wish to actualize your higher purpose on Earth, it is helpful for you to heal yourself at the same time as you develop your intuition. Then you will see clearly through your reality filter. You will view the world through a clean window and consciously connect with your life goals.

Healing Your Aura to Unlock Your Intuition

As a child you were open to possibilities. You were free to use your imagination without limits and envision yourself to be anything you wanted. When I was eleven, I knew I was here to serve as a spiritual teacher. However, I believed this meant I must live like a nun and give up the chance to be wealthy or have a relationship. So I buried this realization and lived in accordance with the expectations of family, culture, and society. I became a PhD microbiologist then a business executive. I traveled the world, chased money and status. One day, I was sitting on the front step of my house when I noticed a bee enjoying a nearby flower. That bee woke me up. I realized that for many years I had not had the time to do a simple thing like appreciate the beauty of a flower. I wondered what had happened to the young child with a realization of her mission and to the grown woman without the time to appreciate nature.

My sudden realization propelled me into an intense period of spiritual growth that transformed my life. I now appreciate that there were three key influencers in my life. Having assisted many others, I am aware the same three things impede us all in the pursuit of happiness and purpose. They cloud your perception like fog. The three influencers are expectations, life challenges, and self-limiting beliefs. Your aura contains a record of the expectations governing your behavior, the beliefs limiting you, and the life challenges that cemented those beliefs. They form your perceptual window that may be cloudy or clear. They are the signal that you transmit to the universe resulting in the life you are living now.

Expectations Impact Your Energy

Expectations can cause you to lose a conscious connection with your unique path. They can come from family, friends, peers, teachers, culture, even religion. When you are being yourself, you are not appreciated. When you behave as they wish, you are validated. When you meet the expectations of others, you are congratulated and encouraged, so you aim to live up to them. You become governed by criticism, judgment, and responsibility, internalizing them and using them to build a false made self, called the ego.

The film *Billy Elliot* is a great example of the pressure we can be under to become someone we are not. In this film, the hero is a little boy who wants to be a ballet dancer. He lives in a mining town where men, including his father, are tough. Billy keeps his true self hidden until it can no longer be contained, and then he must struggle to hold onto himself. We all have a version of the Billy Elliot story inside. Even those who impose expectations on others, like the father and miners in the film, have lost the freedom to accept and be true to themselves.

Life Challenges Affect Your Reality

Life on Earth is a balancing act. From the moment you are born you experience constant cycles of growth and change. You are immersed in a matrix of opposites. If you stray too far to one side of any dichotomy, eventually you will seek to reestablish equilibrium; especially if you feel pain. Emotions, like pain, provide a feedback mechanism. Lower vibration emotions indicate your body is saying you are out of alignment with source. Higher vibration emotions let you know you are aligned with source and on track with what you prefer, and that you are getting along with your body. When in pain, you can believe you are the pain and feel lost. If when facing a challenge, you perceive a threat, you may get stuck in fear and be unable to move forward. You store the pain, fear, and unpleasant experiences in your body and aura.

The original experiences that led to the hate, fear, and pain become embedded in your belief structures. They block the flow of inspiration so that you no longer experience the true light of spirit. It is like living in a house with dusty vents. Ultimately, we create our reality through our beliefs. When we create beliefs that life is difficult, we re-create more painful experiences and our vents get even dustier. Worse, when we have children we pass on our beliefs about a painful limited world to them. The character of Billy Elliot suffered pain from the loss of his mother, the harsh environment in his town, and the financial scarcity and suffering of his family and peers. His clue out of the pain was that dancing made him happy and lifted him above the harsh reality of home.

Your struggle could be relationship problems such as separation, divorce, or never finding a partner. You might need to get your finances sorted out before facing bankruptcy. You might suffer from a chronic and debilitating illness. Perhaps you face challenges such as career uncertainty or job loss or feeling purposeless so you don't know what to do. You crave a vocation that allows you to make a difference but your path seems blocked. You also may be carrying wounds from earlier times when you were abused, bullied, or taunted.

Everyone experiences painful feelings, emotions, and thoughts. There is no person on this Earth who doesn't. Even enlightened spiritual masters experience pain. The difference between them and you is that they have a way of being, or a spiritual practice to ensure that low vibration energy does not stagnate or accumulate. The windows and vents in their houses are kept so clean they see with clarity.

Limiting Beliefs Hold You Back

Self-limiting beliefs cause you to veer from the path of your highest potential. Again, they can originate from family, friends, peers, teachers, culture, and religion. You take on their beliefs to fit in and belong in the group. But if they are not beliefs that are right for you then they hold you back. If Billy Elliot had taken on the macho beliefs of his male role models, he would never have succeeded in performing in the National Ballet. Being a ballet dancer was his true path. Wanting to dance did not make him effeminate or weak. It made him strong, masculine, and free to express his unique essence.

Here are some typical examples of beliefs that hold you back: People like us only ever get so far; I have to work hard for everything I get; I can only have so much; I don't deserve to have what I want; I am unworthy; I have to do everything myself; nobody loves me; there must be something wrong with me.

Knowing what makes you tick is an important step on your path of developing intuition and self-awareness. The early years of life are crucial for the development of your understanding of the world, and the formation of your personality. According to scientists, a newborn brain is 24 percent the size of an adult brain. By age three, it is 80 percent. By five, it is 90 percent. The first three years of life involve rapid growth and learning. Every new experience lays down a neural pathway in the brain. Recurring experiences reinforce and strengthen specific pathways, such as whether you are loved or abused.

Your childhood environment heavily impacts your neural development and your gene expression. From what language you learn to what religious beliefs you hold, early childhood is the time when most behaviors and beliefs are programmed. The biggest influencers are caregivers such as parents, grandparents, aunts, and uncles. They as adults are already programmed. Their environment has led to a set of beliefs about how to behave to stay safe in the world, and they teach these values to you. They already know the surrounding culture and help you orient to their beliefs about religion, social status, country, region, politics, and how to behave correctly. As you get older, you are also influenced by siblings, peers, authority figures such as teachers, and the different groups you get involved in, whether ballet, scouts, or a street gang.

The Process of Getting Unblocked

To be truly yourself you need to break out of your limits. If you cultivate self-awareness by developing your intuition, you will be able to see how you prevent your authentic self from shining through. You can let go of the expectations, challenges, and beliefs that do not serve you. You can validate yourself, what you want and what is possible for you. Intuition opens you to the world of energy. Once you are aware of what you wish to change in your energy field, you can change it using your intentions.

Your intuition will show you who influenced you most strongly through different stages of your life. Then you can let go of their vibrations and replace them with yours. For most of us, this process is like peeling an onion—there are many layers to address. To do it all at once would be overwhelming. Taking your time makes it more comfortable for your body. After all, it took until now to create it! Still, you can clear it faster than you built it up. Developing an intuitive awareness of your aura gives you a framework to follow, because each layer emanates from a different chakra and relates to a different aspect of your life.

Your chakras channel your information and process your life experiences. When stuck, you can move energy through them and clear your blocks. Like jet engines, the chakras fuel your progress and help you head in a certain direction. They allow higher guidance and energy to flow to you from your source. When life challenges restrict the flow of energy through your chakras, you can feel cut off from source, not on your path and out of alignment. Meditation is an effective tool to support you in creating change in your chakras and energy body. It can help you bypass the intellect and emotions that get hijacked by the ego. By learning to be intuitively aware of and work with the energy flowing through your aura and chakras, you can reclaim your power and use your spiritual gifts to create the life you want!

Chapter 4
YOUR CHAKRAS

Imagine you are a star, emitting rays of light throughout the universe. One of your light beams bounces off a small blue planet on a minor spiral arm of the Milky Way galaxy. You catch a glimpse of a beautiful world you wish to explore. Made of dense physical matter, its energy is slowed down. It doesn't obey the same laws of reality you are used to. It has time and space, and everything requires effort to change.

You wonder how to experience it fully and are inspired to create a body for exploring it from the natural materials on the planet. You send yourself to explore Earth, just as NASA sent the Mars Rover to traverse the terrain on Mars. You want your body to operate independently so you store information in it and develop a sensory apparatus capable of interacting with the environment. You remain available to guide it and assign an aspect of your consciousness to stay with it. Clear communication is tantamount, so you install a relay system. Now you can transmit and receive energy signals to and from your body.

In this fun analogy, your chakras are the communication conduits between the higher aspects of yourself (star) and the body personality (Mars Rover) version of yourself.

Your chakras are part of the book of you. They store your beliefs and experiences. They are nonphysical channels that exchange energy and information between higher aspects of you and your body personality, including intuitive abilities. The seven major chakras are positioned along the spine. Each is a channel for spiritual information relating to a different aspect of your reality. They are associated with the endocrine and nervous systems, and direct energy flows through your body. There are also hundreds of additional minor chakras associated with smaller nerve clusters throughout the body. You access your intuition through your chakras. By tuning in to them you can receive your higher guidance, so you can be consciously aware of your current reality and life purpose. By mastering them you can live your purpose. The journey to be a master balancer of chakra energy involves growth and challenges, which differ depending on each specific chakra.

Many systems have been used to explain chakras. In medieval times, there were seven deadly sins and virtues. Chakras were associated with the forces of the gods, planets, archangels, and rays of light. These were ways of illustrating the qualities and challenges associated with each chakra. They were also enigmatically called churches, candlesticks, lamps, vials, seals, and trumpets in the Book of Revelation. While it is commonly understood they must be cleansed and cleared for a healthy body, their relationship with intuition and spiritual development has been shrouded in mystery for centuries.

Chakras and Spiritual Information

Chakras are conduits for your higher wisdom to flow from your source to you. You can consciously access your spiritual information through them to guide your life journey. They also process your life experiences and help you respond. You can cleanse them to stay clear and change their content based on new revelations about your reality. Table 2 shows the spiritual information in the main chakras.

Chakra	Name	Position	Information
First	Root	Near the base of your spine	Survival of the body and human species
Second	Sacral	Two finger widths below your navel	Emotions and sexuality
Third	Solar Plexus	Under your diaphragm	Energy distribution and out-of-body experience

Chakra	Name	Position	Information
Fourth	Heart	Near your heart	Oneness and affinity with self and others
Fifth	Throat	At the cleft of your throat	Communication
Sixth	Brow/ Third Eye	In the center of your brow	Seeing what is
Seventh	Crown	On the crown of your head	Knowing what is

Table 2: Summary of Chakra Information

Each chakra gives a different perspective or vantage point. It can be useful to think of them as windows of perception or doorways of consciousness. Each one helps you appreciate different aspects of reality. Your interpretation of all life situations depends on which window you look through and what information you have stored in it. With a first chakra perspective, you look through your survival instinct lens. With a second chakra viewpoint, you may be filtering your experiences through your sexuality and emotionality.

You can spend lifetimes exploring reality through each level of perception. Your journey, perspective, and way to explore your chakras is as unique as your personal contribution to the symphony of souls and divine creation. Each chakra offers challenges and growth experiences. The lower chakras give you a more physical viewpoint. If you live life looking through these windows, you can lose yourself in the Earth game and forget you are spirit entirely. Focusing exclusively on the upper chakras can make you lose touch with this reality and your body. Unsealing the secrets of all the chakras gives you a balanced perspective. It is necessary to travel through all seven perspectives to truly understand yourself and awaken to your full potential.

We often store other people's concepts in our chakras. It is necessary to purify the chakra system so your unique energy and light of consciousness are expressed. The path of the intuitive involves becoming a master cleanser and balancer of your chakras as well as a master interpreter of your inner guidance system. This path is an ancient route to awakening your divinity while remaining in a human body.

The chakras increase in frequency as you travel up the spine. From the front, chakras look like spinning wheels of light; from the side, they are like horizontal cones with the narrow end pointing to the spine. The only exception is the seventh chakra, which is cylindrical and perpendicular to the ground. Some spiritual systems orient the first chakra vertically with the wide end pointing to the ground and the crown chakra as a funnel with the top open to the universe. Operating them this way can stimulate out-of-body experiences. As this book aims to help you experience life while in your body, orienting your first chakra horizontal to the ground and being aware of using the crown to access your unique information is recommended.

Figure 1 illustrates the positions of the seven main chakras in the body. The first chakra is the one nearest the base of the spine and the seventh chakra is on the crown of the head.

Chakras and the Nervous System

Chakras are places where energy is exchanged between you and your body. All chakras are located near bundles of nerves, which act as the body's electrical system. Your nervous system is a complex arrangement of fibers and neurons that transmit electrical impulses around your body. Your chakras and energy pathways relate to these signaling superhighways yet they are nonphysical conduits for your energy. They are not part of the physical system. They are part of your spiritual energy system.

The metaphor of petals, increasing in number from the first to seventh chakra, is often used to show an increase in vibration as well as the number of nerves in the corresponding plexus.[13] Nerves in each plexus communicate with body parts nearby. Edgar Cayce said the twelve pairs of cranial nerves leading to the five senses are significant in body spirit communication.[14] They also correspond with a series of minor chakras in the head (see Table 3).

13. Borsboom, Wim. The Chakras and their Petals—A Technical Overview. http://thekund aliniprocess.blogspot.com/. Accessed April 2019.

14. Auken, John. Edgar Cayce on the Revelation: A Study Guide for Spiritualizing Body and Mind. New York: Sterling, 2005.

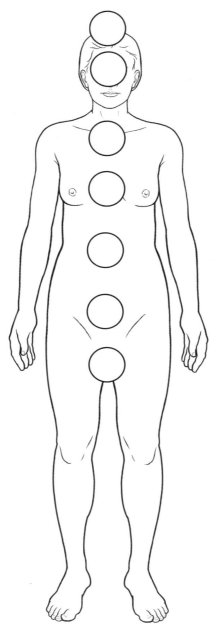

Figure 1: Positions of the chakras in the body

Chakra	Nerve Plexus	Position/Vertebra	Petals	Nerve Pairs
First	Sacral-coccygeal	L4-L5	4	2
Second	Lumbar	L1-L3	6	3
Third	Solar	T8-T12	10	5
Fourth	Cardiac	T2-T7	12	6
Fifth	Pharyngeal	C1-C7+T1	16	8
Sixth	Carotid	Head	2	1
Seventh	Cranial	Brain	1000	12

Table 3: Chakras and Nerve Plexi

Chakras and the Endocrine System

The chakras are intimately connected to the body's endocrine system, which comprises glands and glandular tissues as well as the hormones they release. These chemical messengers are carried around by the bloodstream and regulate the activities of the organs and tissues they target. There are more than seven glands, but as a general guide, the chakras are positioned close to the glands they stimulate. There are varied opinions for chakras 1, 2 and 3. Table 4 shows these relationships as given by Edgar Cayce in his translation of the Book of Revelations.

Chakra	Gland	Hormone Function
First	Gonads	Reproduction, sexual differentiation (androgens, estrogen, progesterone)
Second	Lyden	Gestation of a body created via coition (not yet known)
Third	Adrenal Cortex (and pancreas)	Glucose, sodium, potassium metabolism (steroids/insulin and glucagon for the pancreas)
Third or First	Adrenal Medulla	Fight or flight (epinephrine/sympathetic nerve response

Chakra	Gland	Hormone Function
Fourth	Thymus	Immune function (T-cells development hormones)
Fifth	Thyroid	Metabolic rate; heart, weight, energy use (T1, T2, thyroxin)
Sixth	Pineal	Body rhythms, sleep, sexual development (melatonin)
Seventh	Pituitary	Master gland (many hormones)

Table 4: Chakras and Endocrine Function

Your pineal gland is a receiver and transmitter of light. It is able to receive the multidimensional language of spirit. By placing your consciousness in this seat of the soul you become divine man. From this perspective, you can consciously operate as spirit through a human body. The pituitary gland is the lieutenant of the pineal gland. It translates signals from the pineal into action in the body by interacting with the nervous and endocrine systems. These systems meet in the hypothalamus, which is part of the thalamus. The thalamus is a hub that processes and relays sensory input to other parts of the brain. Metaphysically speaking, the thalamus is associated with the crown chakra, which brings your energy into the body. The hypothalamus links the nervous and endocrine systems together. It is a cluster of nerve cells that produce regulatory hormones that travel to the pituitary gland, which sends hormonal signals to the rest of the endocrine system.

This structure of body-spirit communication was known in ancient Egypt as the Eye of Horus. It has also been referred to as the horn of the Unicorn, the third eye of Shiva, the place of the Alchemical Wedding, and other mystical names. Spirit has access to the entire body through the pineal gland, pituitary, and hypothalamus. You have access to your higher self through this gateway of consciousness. Spirit is also intimately connected to each organ, cell, DNA strand, and all the molecules and atoms and subatomic particles of matter. There is a network of minor chakras and energy lines that underpin the physical projection of the body. You interact with your body and the multidimensional quantum field through these aspects of spirit.

The adrenal glands are associated with the first and third chakras, because there are two different functions of the adrenals. One relates to the fight or flight survival response and the other to metabolism and energy distribution. Similarly, in humans the gonads ensure species survival, and the sex organs also relate to creative power. According to Cayce, there is a small gland (Lyden) in the belly yet to be discovered by science. It is a channel for life force and is responsible for the creation of the human body during gestation. He describes it as a seat of consciousness as important as the pineal gland.

Chakras and Spiritual Growth

As spirit you exist outside of time and space; you operate with no effort. When you make changes as spirit they are instant. Your body, however, exists in time and space and uses effort and energy to function. It needs time and space to adjust to change. As you guide your body through its journey and help it navigate the world of form, you must be patient. Your intuition can help by giving you insights about your body's growth and your life challenges, so as to make your journey more pleasant.

Applying your intuition to read your chakras provides useful information about your life experiences as well as how you can release your blocks and live a consciously purposeful life. As you receive higher information and process your life experiences through your chakras, being able to intuitively sense their vibration, spin, energy flow, and openness can help you understand yourself and life more deeply. Being able to modulate them can help you heal and balance your energy.

Doing this regularly can help you observe and guide your life journey from a spiritual perspective. Being aware of where you are in all areas of life, yet also seeing your power to create and move through challenges, can be a great comfort. Sometimes you might be more focused on physical reality. If you are going through a growth cycle related to survival, whether it's a health or financial matter, you will have more emphasis on your first chakra and its information. Another time you could be seeking answers about your personal concept of divinity, so more of your attention may be on your seventh chakra, where you are accessing your higher knowing, or on removing deluding beliefs from your sixth chakra to see more clearly.

Realizing this can help you relax, accept where you are, and enjoy your growth process. Otherwise, you could expect to be in a different spiritual, mental, emotional, or physical place. You might expect to be healthy when you are ill, rich when you are poor, or all knowing when you have no answers. There is no perfect way to be. All life experiences are valid and spiritual growth cycles come in many forms. Each chakra governs a different aspect of life. Changes made as spirit in any area of life lead to adjustments in your body and physical reality. When you resist changing, your energy flow may become restricted or blocked. Then your body may become mentally, emotionally, or physically disturbed.

First Chakra

Your root chakra provides your support system for living in physical reality. It channels information on survival of the human body and species. This includes maintaining health, and creating abundance and balance in a world of opposites. The first chakra governs biological and physiological needs such as air, food, drink, shelter, warmth, sleep, and sex for species survival. The energy that emanates from your first chakra forms part of your aura. Reading it can help you understand your state of being at this level of reality. Learning how to operate consciously as spirit through your body is a major part of your purpose. Your first chakra also contains information on how to heal your body and use your unique male and female energy to create your reality. By mastering your first chakra, you have the foundation of support you need to focus on your unique contribution. If you ground from this energy center, you create a stable platform for life. By owning, balancing, and consciously operating it, you get to heal and create the life you want.

Most humans today are trapped in survival games and operate mostly from this plane of reality. If you are in a first chakra growth cycle, you may experience challenges relating to survival. This could manifest as poor health or lack of money. Or it could be that you desire change in the form of a new job, creative project, or another form of physical self-expression. Making this change might require an adjustment in how you organize your life. The body might respond by needing sleep, exercise, or dietary changes. If you resist by keeping it awake, being inactive, or force-feeding it junk, it may be uncooperative, become emotional, or create a physical ailment. Examples of someone in a first chakra growth cycle resisting change could be a stressed-out businessman who develops cancer while facing bankruptcy or a homeless woman escaping into drugs, sleeping in a tent, and begging for food. Both are facing survival challenges. Both may desire change and rearrange their beliefs to heal their situations.

Second Chakra

Your sacral chakra contains your information on emotions, sexuality, and creative expression. The form of intuition located in the second chakra is known as clairsentience. This sense of clear feeling allows you to feel the emotions and sexuality of yourself and others. It can be helpful to think of this energy center as the human relationship chakra. The energy that emanates from it forms a layer of your aura that relates to these aspects. Many humans are caught up in cycles of pain and suffering from creating dissatisfying relationships with others and life situations that are out of alignment with source. People operating mainly from their second chakra can be driven by emotions and sex. Their self-identity may depend on their relationship with others, and they may not be centered within their own being at all. If you listen to your emotions and sex drive, they will tell you what your body needs to be cooperative.

If you listen to your intuition, it will help you maintain your body's health such as letting go of your dependencies on food, sex, and other people. Spiritual changes that put you in a second chakra growth cycle can involve relationships such as a new baby or lover, learning about your sexuality, or channeling emotional or sexual energy into creative projects. When you take charge of your second chakra, you can balance the needs of your body with your need to serve a higher purpose. By consciously owning and operating your second chakra, you free yourself to choose your purpose as opposed to only responding to the body's instincts. You also give yourself permission to grow beyond the limits of the group and own and express your unique creative vibration instead of merging with others.

Third Chakra

Your solar plexus chakra contains information on energy distribution, including how you focus energy to create your life experiences. It also has information on operating outside of your physical body; it helps you translate information from other dimensional experiences for relevance to this reality. In addition to your human body and Earthly experiences, you have an astral body and astral experiences, where you have more latitude to play out consciousness-expanding games with human friends and other beings. The energy that emanates from your third chakra forms another layer of your auric field. Once you are sufficiently self-aware to know your purpose, owning your third chakra allows you to consciously focus your energy to support your goals on Earth and the astral plane. You have all you need within you to achieve this purpose.

Third chakra growth cycles can deal with self-esteem, status, achievement, independence, dominance, prestige, and responsibility. A third chakra growth cycle can involve learning about power, competition, control, victimization, and self-worth. Sometimes people learn how to use their energy by misusing it. Being lost in this layer offers many possibilities for power games. Being powerful is not the ability to manipulate others; it is claiming your energy and using it to create the life you want. You can set boundaries by owning your third chakra and use your energy how you want rather than be intimidated by fear to give your energy and power away to others.

Fourth Chakra

Your fourth chakra channels information about oneness and affinity as well as your concepts about unconditional love, compassion, and the ability to give and receive. When this center is balanced, you can appreciate yourself, other people, and their creations. As it is located near the heart, it is also called the heart chakra. Positioned between the lower three chakras and the upper three chakras, it balances the physical and spiritual realms within you. The field of energy emanated from the fourth chakra bridges consciousness between your upper and lower centers, giving you an appreciation of the oneness from the perspective of individuality and duality. To heal and know your fourth chakra opens the window to feel your passion for your higher purpose. It also helps you to appreciate where you fit in the world. An open heart chakra can guide your direction and help you attract what you need to pursue and fulfill your life purpose.

A fourth chakra growth cycle may challenge you to move through judgment and non-forgiveness to acceptance of self and others. It can also manifest as confusion between sex, emotions, and love. Or mixing up oneness with physical togetherness, causing you to merge energy with others and lose your unique perspective. Many spiritual teachings emphasize being heart-centered; being above a physical individuated focus is perceived as a virtue. Yet this can cause loss of individuality if it becomes your sole focus to the exclusion of other chakras. Then you miss out on one of the best parts of having a body on Earth.

Fifth Chakra

Your throat chakra governs authentic communication. Physical communication includes speech, hearing, and self-expression. It alerts you to what is going on in the physical reality and allows communication with others. If your fifth chakra is unbalanced, you may feel uninspired, be unclear about your message, fear speaking out, or be a poor communicator. As you clear the beliefs causing this, you will grow as a communicator. Spiritual communication lets you know what is going on in your spiritual reality. It includes broad and narrowband telepathy, clairaudience, inner voice, and pragmatic intuition. These abilities allow you to communicate at a higher frequency range than your normal senses.

In this information age, there is so much communication. Spiritual teachings are even being spread over the internet. It can be confusing to discern which teachers to listen to and what information to believe. All of your information is within you. Mastering the fifth chakra can help you open your inner voice so you can be clear about your unique information. Then you can speak and live your truth. Your fifth chakra helps you communicate with your higher self, body, source, other humans, and nonphysical beings from other realities. By mastering it, you can consciously choose to listen to a preferred angel or guide over an unhelpful being. As you own it, you may feel inspired, be more creative, and communicate more clearly. Your personal goals and higher service will be supported by clearer communication with your inner voice, higher guides, and source.

Sixth Chakra

Your brow chakra channels your information on clairvoyance and abstract intuition. These abilities allow you to perceive colors, shapes, vibrations, and frequencies of energy in this reality and in other realities. The pineal gland, located in the center of your head and sixth chakra, is a receptacle of light. You are light and the pineal gland is where you are meant to sit within your body. When you place your consciousness here, you can see clearly from a neutral, nonjudgmental perspective and you begin to stimulate your clairvoyance. When you own this chakra, you can have your neutrality. It is easier to love and heal yourself from this nonjudgmental perspective. You can see and accept people, situations, and life creations clearly. You can easily move on from what you don't prefer when you are not in judgment or resistance.

A sixth chakra growth cycle might include difficulty focusing, lack of clarity, mental health issues, or fuzzy thinking. You might view the world through a filter of unsupportive beliefs, be inundated by unwanted visions, or not see anything at all. Your sixth chakra helps you to have clarity about your higher purpose. When you see clearly about yourself, others, your body, emotions, and intellect, then you can take charge of your reality. You can release limits and then direct your energy to focus on what you want to do. Another name for the sixth chakra mastery is Christ Consciousness. When fully owned, the third eye allows you to perceive nonphysical beings and communicate with them via the language of color and symbol. You can appreciate the divine nature of all souls and communicate with them through love and acceptance.

Seventh Chakra

Your seventh chakra is the place where you the spiritual being can enter your body. It has information on how you can channel your own or other's energy. It connects you to source and higher wisdom. This crown chakra is the master chakra. It receives and transfers information from cosmic consciousness throughout your energy system, including all your other chakras. By taking charge of your seventh chakra, you can consciously enter your physical body and direct your life from your higher consciousness. You can communicate with source and receive guidance and answers to your questions.

If you do not gain seniority over this center, you may live your life unconsciously or possessed by energies and beliefs that are not yours. An unbalanced seventh chakra can lead to misconceptions, frustration, and unrealized potential. When this chakra awakens, you may be amazed at how much you know. It can be challenging not to lose yourself in the enormity of what is or impose your information on others. Remember, everyone is unique and can access their own information; and information that is appropriate for you may not resonate with others. As the seventh chakra allows direct connection to the divine, having a balanced seventh chakra will help you know who you are and why you are here. It can help you understand your life challenges and your purpose, and provide guidance as you progress along your life journey.

Balance Your Chakras to Balance Your Life

Your chakras work together as an integrated whole. When they're in harmony it is easier to feel fulfilled and purposeful. As you live on a planet of duality, your life experiences constantly move between different polarities. Your chakras help you navigate these variances and regain balance between opposing forces. If an imbalance is ignored and becomes longstanding, it can lead to physical dysfunction. A disease that develops near a chakra usually corresponds to an imbalance in that chakra. For example, thyroid problems relate to the fifth chakra. Mental health issues to the seventh chakra. Heart problems to the fourth chakra and so on.

You will have many growth cycles in a lifetime. Look back over your life to see the cycles of physical and spiritual change you have experienced. As long as you have a physical body you will experience growth, change, and expansion. Depending on what is happening in your life and what the emphasis of your current spiritual growth is, there will be a heavier focus on chakras that relate more to your growth. Plus, there will be a response in your body to the change. You might have a dominant chakra or operate principally from one or two chakras while you adjust. During your growth cycle, you can experience the world and interact with others predominantly from the perspective of those chakras.

Chakra	Body
First/Root	Hips, legs, lower back, adrenals
Second/Sacral	Kidneys, gonads, bladder, large intestine, mid back
Third/Solar Plexus	Stomach, liver, gall bladder, pancreas, small intestine, digestion, upper mid back
Fourth/Heart	Heart, lungs, thymus, circulation, shoulders, upper back
Fifth/Throat	Throat, neck, teeth, ears, mouth, thyroid gland
Sixth/Brow	Eyes, face, brain, lymphatic system, pineal gland
Seventh/Crown	Brain, nerves, pituitary, thalamus, hypothalamus

Table 5: Chakras and Physical Organs

The relationship between chakras and health is a popular topic yet little has been written on their role as channels for communication to provide access to your higher senses. The purpose of this book isn't to provide indepth information on chakras and health. Instead, it is to help you understand chakras in the context of your spiritual guidance system and communication conduits for your higher information.

Chakra Growth Cycles

Your life challenges and growth cycles can be clues to your intuition style. If your difficulties relate to lack of abundance or ill health, you are dealing with your first chakra and its survival instinct. If you have emotional issues and trouble setting boundaries, you are working on owning your second chakra and clairsentience. If your energy is scattered, you're facing power struggles, or feel unfocused or like you are disassociated from your body, your third chakra and its aspects are at play. If you lack passion or feel lonely or rejected, you are learning about your heart's affinity and oneness. If your challenges relate to communication, you could be clearing blocks to using spiritual abilities within your fifth chakra. Not seeing clearly, or not accepting what is, means your growth cycle relates to your sixth chakra and its aspect of clairvoyance. Being a know-it-all or giving seniority to others means you are being challenged to clear your crown chakra and develop your knowingness. For more information about chakras and spiritual growth, I recommend *Chakras: Key to Spiritual Opening* by Mary Ellen Flora.[15]

SIGNIFICANT LIFE CHALLENGES EXERCISE

Follow the clues your life experiences give you about your spiritual abilities by completing this exercise:

1. Make a list of your most significant life challenges. Write as many as you remember in as much detail as you can.
2. Identify which chakra(s) were involved for each life challenge.
3. Notice common themes or trends that relate to certain chakras over others.

Keep these notes handy as you will need them again in Part Three.

15. Flora, Mary Ellen. *Chakras: Key to Spiritual Opening.* Everett: CDM Publications, 1999.

Chapter 5
BLOCKS TO INTUITION

Before you identify your intuition style, it helps to appreciate how you might be blocking it. This chapter covers the most common barriers people encounter regardless of their intuition style or where they are on their intuition journey. It also discusses how meditation can help overcome these blocks. In Part Two, we will explore challenges that relate to specific types of intuition, and in Part Three, we will learn meditation techniques for intuition development. Then you can use meditation to release these limits and quiet external reality so you can hear your messages.

For now, let's explore what limits you may be encountering, including these seven major blocks.

1. Being Too Busy

People who wish to develop intuition ask me how they can find time to meditate given their responsibilities. Or they say they get fidgety or fall asleep due to exhaustion when they meditate. If you have a demanding job, family members who rely on you, and a tendency to take on too much, you may be run off your feet and suffer from anxiety. Perhaps you also believe you don't have time to develop your intuition.

Sometimes the stress of being too busy becomes a physical symptom and is medicated. The good news is meditation has been scientifically proven to eliminate stress, calm the mind, increase focus, and heal illness. Rather than taking up your time, it helps you practice self-awareness and manage your time and energy more effectively. If you identify as having a busy life, please consider that you may have a misperception of busyness because your energy is spread too thinly.

There are three main ways we inappropriately spread out our energy. First is not being present: If you keep getting stuck in the past or are focused on the future, you will have the illusion of being busier than you are. Think about the difference between having your focus in a single moment versus spread over many moments. Second is giving your energy away by taking responsibility for others and prioritizing their needs above yours. This means you will always be chasing your tail and never complete what you want to do. Third is having an untrained mind constantly thinking random thoughts or obsessing over your to-do list, which will cause you to believe you are busy. Actually, it is just your mind that is inappropriately busy.

2. Too Much Mind Chatter

The Buddha imagined the human mind was filled with drunken monkeys who jumped around constantly chattering. I frequently hear from people who can't turn their busy mind off sufficiently to access their intuition. They have enough issues concentrating in daily life, let alone focusing in meditation. If you want to know how to cultivate a peaceful mind where the subtle signals of your intuition can be heard, I recommend you learn to meditate. Meditation is crucial to help you calm your mind; it puts your monkeys to sleep. Take a moment to examine your thought patterns. If you are like most people, you will discover you hold onto the past, obsess about the future, keep repeatedly reviewing your to-do list, regurgitate the same old stuff, and are caught in cycles of self-criticism and judgment.

It's also common to get confused between the mind, body, brain, ego, soul, and spirit. Your mind is part of your body. Your thoughts occur in the cerebral cortex of your brain, which is a physical organ. Allowing your mind to flutter is like letting a horse ride itself. Your thoughts arise from your ego or even other egos. When you have an untrained mind that constantly thinks random thoughts, you are not operating as spiritual consciousness. You are not in charge; your body is. Meditation can help you tune out distractions, be the neutral observer of your thoughts, and focus in present time on what is occurring now. You don't need to escape to the mountaintop like gurus of old. You just need to take charge as spirit. Grab the reins so you can reap the benefits of a calmer mind. A calm mind can help you live a peaceful life, have a sense of well-being, and be more joyful. It can also help you concentrate, sleep better, and be more accepting.

3. Roller-Coaster Emotions

Some people's lives are an emotional roller-coaster ride. If they aren't having a meltdown, then someone close is. I met a woman who said she could not meditate to access her intuition because she could not calm down. She did not know meditation was the solution to her problem. If you wish you knew how to cope with emotional overwhelm, if you feel drained by others, or if you have uncontrollable fear, anger, grief, sadness, or impatience, meditation is your answer. Once you calm your emotions, you can sense your intuition. It's the difference between a stormy day on the ocean when you can't see farther than the deck of the boat versus a clear, sunny day where you can see the far horizon and everything between.

If you fear what will come up as you develop your intuition, you are not alone. It is a common concern to wonder if you can deal with what you might become aware of. If you worry about emotional trauma from the past overwhelming you, please believe me when I say meditation can help you release your trauma without re-experiencing it. Emotional overwhelm and dramatic outbursts are no fun. Emotions are your body's communication system. Allowing them to dominate is like letting a toddler rule the roost instead of the parent. Let go of confusion about emotions. Validate you are spirit, so you can receive emotional feedback from your body as it experiences your life situations. If you don't listen and take charge, your body will.

Meditation helps you communicate with your body. It gives you control over lower vibration emotions such as fear, anger, hate, irritability, and anxiety, and it gives you the ability to channel more positive emotional vibrations. You don't need to fight your body, though that might happen to begin with depending on how much you have let emotions rule your reality. You just need to take charge as spirit, steer your body through the emotional ups and downs. Then you will reap the benefits of a calmer body, which include better relationships, resilience to change, improved boundaries, less resistance to foreign energy, clarity about what you want, and freedom to focus on your life path.

4. Trying Too Hard

"Going into" effort is a big block to receiving your intuitive insights. When you use effort, your body is trying to do it for you. It's an easy trap to fall into, especially as we are so programmed to let the intellect dominate. But the intellect is a function of your brain and you are spirit. If you wonder why your intuition isn't working, it could be because you are trying too hard. Gurus, books, workshops, videos, talismans, incense, crystals, totems, card decks or other spiritual paraphernalia will not help you if you are in effort.

All you need to access your intuition is a consistent meditation practice and a good teacher. Unfortunately, a lot of the learning material available keeps you in your intellect. Everything in physical reality takes effort. As your body is physical, everything it does, such as thinking, exercising, breathing, and digesting food, uses energy. It follows then that your body is dominating your spiritual journey if you are struggling to be spiritual or intuitive. Remember, you are not your body. Your consciousness operates outside of time and space in nonphysical reality. Nothing you do takes effort, including using intuition.

From now on when you experience effort, you will know that is not your high vibration consciousness. You will realize it is your body using effort to get things done. Your spiritual unfolding is not being controlled by the ego, mind, body, or emotions. It is being guided by spirit. By releasing effort you get out of your own way. Reflect on your journey so far, notice where you get into effort and let it go. Opening intuition equals choosing to release effort and operate consciously as spirit. Meditation can help you discern body and spirit and release effort so spirit can take charge of your life journey. This will help you feel more in charge, relaxed, in the flow of life, and connected with source.

5. Striving for Spiritual Perfectionism

Do you have ideas about what intuition should be like? One woman told me she was expecting literal lightning bolts and was very disappointed when it wasn't like that. Expectations make you judge, criticize, and compare yourself to people you believe have perfected themselves. Conversely, if you think you are the brilliant one, you might wonder why you haven't been recognized yet as one of the special humans with psychic powers. What's more, if you expect only to see dead people or auras, you might miss the guidance from your inner voice or your angels when they sing to you.

In this world of instant gratification, people want instant results. Meditation is viewed as a time waster if it doesn't deliver on their expectations immediately. This is why we now have so many apps delivering instant snappy meditations. Put on your inner chef now. Calm down in five minutes. Be your best self in an instant. While these apps popularize meditation and make it accessible, they also create a fast-food mentality about it. The path of the intuitive requires commitment and the courage to know yourself deeply, including what you swept under the carpet during your life. This takes time. Meditation is a lifestyle choice, and if you use it to clean up your energy field, you will reap the rewards you seek.

Pause here to ask whether you have expectations of your spiritual journey, or judgments about being worthy or unworthy. Expectations stop you fully experiencing what is. They stop you accepting yourself as you are in the present moment. You don't need to be perfect, change to fit in, or pretend to be someone you aren't. There is no other person like you. Let your unique style of intuition emerge naturally and celebrate its uniqueness.

Meditation helps you let go of expectations and accept yourself. It can free you of perfectionism, competition, and unworthiness so you can love who you are versus who you think you should be. No one else can do the job of being you. In the words of Oscar Wilde, "Be yourself; everyone else is already taken." The original is better than a copy, so give us the gift of your unique note in the symphony of humanity. You will gain yourself and your unique relationship with source energy. There is nothing worth exchanging for that. Be patient and give yourself time to get to know yourself more deeply and accept yourself unconditionally.

6. Uncertainty, Doubt, and Fear

When people do set time aside for their intuition, some are plagued with uncertainty and invalidate what they get. Even when they meditate, they aren't sure if they're doing it correctly. They are afraid they are wrong and even more afraid they are right. Common fears I encounter include fear of failure, losing touch with reality, seeing scary things, and being called crazy or evil—as well as fears of being unable to cope with one's power and potential, experiencing past pain, and the reactions of loved ones.

It is true that sometimes you may be aware of things that make you uncomfortable or wish weren't true. Meditation can help you to be neutral about what comes up and release it. Most people have been so invalidated and disempowered they no longer believe in their ability to cope. Meditation can help you clear the invalidation and open a door for you to see your beauty and divinity.

Ask yourself what you are afraid of when it comes to intuition and personal growth. The fear itself is always worse than what is feared. Fear of loneliness is worse than being alone, and fear of suffering can be worse than the actual suffering itself. Fear of the future is worse than being present. Perhaps our most innate bodily fear is fear of death, but when you think about it, this is worse than dying. When you have been afraid of making a change, I bet you wondered what you were worried about once you moved through it.

Another big fear is of our potential. Meditation can help you release it and experience your brightness. Intuition helps you access your light and frees you from your inner darkness. Fear keeps you frozen. There can be no progress when there is fear. If you have things you want to do, you must eliminate fear to achieve it. The opposite of being afraid is letting your light shine. There are so many benefits I could not list them here. Nothing compares to being self-loving, knowing your brightness and following your passion. Susan Jeffers was correct when she wrote *Feel the Fear and Do It Anyway*. Be courageous, and what you are scared of will dissolve and you will be free.

7. Not Trusting Your Intuition

Many of us pride ourselves on our logical approach to life. The intellect is a powerful tool that keeps us safe and helps us find a place in society. Both ego and intellect can be challenging when it comes to tuning in to your intuition. Often people can't validate their intuition because of it. They can't tell the difference between their brain, ego, soul, and intuition. They let the ego self-sabotage and override their intuition. To have faith in your intuition, you must first recognize it. Then you can end your confusion and trust it.

The intellect belongs to your body and is part of your brain. Your ego includes your inner critic, outer judge, emotional triggers, and more. It can sabotage your intuition in a misguided attempt to protect you, or to keep you stuck in a physical reality perspective. Eckhart Tolle calls the false made self the pain body.[16] If you have identified with it, you will see the world through a distorted lens. Your intuition will be wonky. You must peel back the layers of illusion and remove baggage to see your reality more clearly. If you are unclear which voice is speaking or if you are afraid your ego is tricking you by overriding your intuition, meditation can help you be discerning and set your ego aside.

MY INTUITION BLOCKS EXERCISE

Reflect on which of the seven blocks to developing intuition you resonate with most. On a page in your notebook, draw a line down the center so you have two columns. List the seven blocks in the left column, and then give yourself a score between 0 and 3 for each (0 for not affected by this block at all, 1 for mildly impacted, 2 for impacted, and 3 for extremely impacted).

If you have a total score between 0 and 7, then you are doing well. Between 7 and 14 indicates that there are some issues to overcome. If your score is between 14 and 21, then you have some work to do. For all these scores, the meditation exercises presented in Part Three will help you significantly.

Acting on Your Intuition

It is possible to acknowledge intuition yet not act on it. Even after overcoming doubts, transcending limits, and building confidence in it, you can still have a problem following it. Taking action can be scary, especially if you were taught to look before you leap. Luckily, you can use your intuition to clear what is causing your procrastination. Reasons why we resist our guidance include being influenced by someone else, having low self-esteem, and having self-limiting beliefs.

---

16. Tolle, Eckhart. *The Power of Now: A Guide to Spiritual Enlightenment.* Vancouver: Namaste Publishing, 2004.

Being Influenced by Others

I know capable people who struggle to act on their intuition due to concern of how it will impact others. If you are afraid of disappointing someone, you may think twice about following your intuition. Caring what others think leaves you vulnerable. Others may manipulate you. Due to their fear of change, they prefer you remain the same. They don't want you examining your life because they don't want to be scrutinized. They hope you won't see clearly as they don't want to be seen. Instead of allowing things to unfold, they try to control them. When people are scared, their energy can invade your energy field, triggering emotional reactions, confused thoughts, and lack of clarity, making it hard to tap into your intuition, let alone follow it.

When you care about someone, it can be tempting to sacrifice your happiness to keep the peace. You don't help anyone by being a martyr, but the whole world will benefit when you follow your calling. You are unique. When you play small you don't serve the world, you prevent us benefitting from your gifts. You have to own your energetic space to follow your higher guidance. The more you own your space the more you are aware of what you want, can see yourself and others clearly, and are able to move forward unimpeded.

It is true that following your intuition might disturb or displease others. Upsetting someone's apple cart can cause unpleasant repercussions. That person might pile on guilt and responsibility or make fun of you. If you are a people pleaser, learn to trust your intuition and follow what is right for you. Dare to differ. Don't listen to those who want you to be like them so they feel better about themselves. Clear out the naysayers. Validate yourself, your intuition, and your power to make good life choices.

Suffering from a Lack of Self-Esteem

Low self-esteem is one of the biggest reasons people deny themselves and ignore their intuition. If you feel unworthy to receive, you will deny your dreams and be unhappy. There is much abuse in our world. Whether emotional, mental, sexual, or physical, it is impossible to find a human who hasn't been abused. Even well-meaning parents have projections about who they want you to be. Without meaning to be cruel, they can inadvertently teach you it isn't all right to be you.

Abuse leads to unworthiness; whether expressed as a shrinking violet, dominating sociopath, limelight-seeking narcissist, or ordinary person lacking confidence. Sensitive people feel different, and experience loneliness. They don't fit in with their family and culture, and they have difficulty finding like-minded people. As a result, they become isolated or turn down their light to merge with the group for a sense of belonging.

All humans experience feelings of unworthiness at some point but there are various ways we respond. One way is to become an abuser. Another is to live in denial. A third option is to see our truth and commit to a path of healing. Intuition can show you how to release unworthiness and recognize your merit. When you don't fit in, you feel lonely, but loneliness denies you are spirit. As a spark of divine consciousness, you can never be outside of creation or cut off from source. Though you can be out of alignment and have the illusion of being alone. By developing your intuition you can experience support from your trusted divine source, angels, and guides and need never feel alone again.

Self-Limiting Beliefs that Keep You Stuck

Following your messages could change your life in ways you feel unprepared for. Your inner guidance may take you in a new direction, involve learning new things, or go against what you have done before. You could experience a battle between body and spirit or intellect and intuition. Your ego being invested in old patterns must be persuaded to support change. Your emotionally triggered inner child needs calming. Your reactionary outer judge has to be cajoled into supporting you. Taking a leap into the unknown can be scary.

Usually when we feel blocked, there is a limiting belief lurking around us. Core beliefs were placed in your energy field early in life, and you've been creating your reality through them. Their energy signature attracts similar experiences, which reinforces them, and the cycle repeats. When intense experiences lead to memories with emotional imprints, the next time a similar event happens, your reaction is disproportionate. While it feels real to you, what is actually happening is you are tapping into emotional layers built up over time.

You don't have to let your past define you. If you take charge as spirit, you can quiet the unsupportive voices. The journey of all humans is to learn to consciously operate as spirit through the body and deal with its intellect, emotions, and ego. When there are stacks of related experiences containing limiting beliefs and emotional triggers, removing the underlying core belief makes it easier to release everything else like a stack of dominos. Be patient, as there can be many blocks, but eventually they will all tumble down.

By focusing on the present moment, you can let go of the past. You can't change it in any way. Cease worrying about the future. If you obsess about it, you fuel your fears. Relax and trust that the universe supports you. What you desire is created the moment you ask for it. All you need do is let go of doubt and receive.

ACTING ON INTUITION EXERCISE

Reflect on how well you respond to your intuition. On a page in your notebook, draw a line down the center so you have two columns. In the left column, list the times you remembered to follow your intuition. In the right column, list the times when you did not follow your intuition. Remember as many incidences as possible.

Now, count the total number of examples in each column. For the times when you did not listen to your higher guidance, make a note if it was because you were influenced by others, had a limiting belief, or were suffering from a lack of confidence. Notice trends where one reason is more predominant than the others. Validate all the times you did follow your intuition. If there is a bigger list of instances where you overrode your intuition, don't despair. The meditation exercises in Part Three will help you to overcome your blocks.

Meditation Unblocks Intuition

As well as the blocks discussed in this chapter, each intuitive gift comes with its own unique challenges. Meditation is the best tool to use for overcoming them; it is crucial to developing intuition as it helps you:

- Remove core beliefs that block you.
- Quiet your mind so you can focus.

- Calm your emotions and be neutral.
- De-stress from your busy life.
- Release effort and distinguish it from your ego.
- Let go of your expectations and perfectionism.
- Overcome doubt, fear, and unworthiness.
- Validate, trust and follow your intuition.
- Develop your intuition so you can use it as you wish.

Meditation has also been scientifically shown to have benefits in the physical, emotional, mental, and spiritual aspects of life. Studies have shown that meditation can elevate immunity, improve pain management, decrease heart rate and blood pressure, improve sleep and digestion, increase energy, and speed up recovery time from illness. There has also been much research to confirm the power of meditation to relieve and manage stress. People who meditate have been shown to be less irritable. It alleviates anxiety and reduces depression, which leads to improved interpersonal relationships and resilience to change. Meditation can enhance brain function, intelligence, and memory. It can improve your decision-making ability.

For thousands of years, shamans and spiritual masters have used meditation to access the unseen world and seek guidance from higher consciousness. Meditation is the one sure way for you to open your intuition and connect with your divine nature and spiritual information. All in all, there is much to incentivize you to practice meditation and little reason not to. Yet I encounter many people who find it difficult to sustain a regular meditation practice. The reasons why they cannot meditate are similar to the reasons why they cannot access their intuition:

- My mind will not shut up long enough to meditate.
- I can't sit still; my body needs to keep moving.
- I am in a constant state of emotional turbulence.
- If I don't see results immediately, I want to quit.
- My body hurts or I fall asleep.
- I try but I question if I am doing it right.
- My life is too busy; I can't find the time.

The most important one to crack is the last one. Once you develop a consistent practice, meditation will help alleviate the other reasons. You will see for yourself how much meditation helps you and you will be empowered to overcome all of them. If you were training for a triathlon, you would not get far at the event if you did not train every day. Meditation is like this. It works best when practiced daily, whether you are doing it for relaxation or intuition development. If you want the benefits of a quiet mind, calm emotions, releasing effort, and connecting with your intuition, you need to find a meditation style that works for you.

There are lots of styles of meditation available. I practice and teach a style that was taught in the ancient mystery schools. These teachings were revitalized in modern times by my teacher, Mary Ellen Flora, and others. I also incorporate techniques that my guides suggest. Some have lived on Earth and used mystery practices while others bring new ideas, expanded awareness, and amusement.

If you are attracted to this book, it could be that you encountered this type of meditation in past lives. (This was my experience.) Reading this book, then, will help you remember what you already know and show you how to use it in present time.

My meditation form includes tools for a solid foundation for life. They activate intuition, allow you to manage your energy, consciously create your reality, cleanse your energy field, and heal your body. I will introduce these meditation mysteries in Part Three. Once you have learned them, you can use them to overcome your intuition challenges.

There is no correct behavior when it comes to following higher guidance. Don't beat yourself up if you ignore it, or if you skip a meditation. Peeling back the layers of the onion takes patience. Be kind. If you have difficulty making a change, ask for it to happen when it is for the highest good of all concerned. Everything unfolds in its own time so take the pressure off. No matter what you do or don't do you will learn and grow. You have lots of time to take action if action is what's needed.

Sometimes you just need to get out of your own way and receive the flow of life. You have free will and so it is up to you what you do with your information. However, going against the flow can put you out of alignment with source and your life may feel off kilter. If you meditate, learn neutrality, and release expectations, you can create and receive changes that make your life more enjoyable.

Be brave. Take a leap of faith. Please yourself and stop putting others first. Own your energy field. Release the past, let go of limiting beliefs, negative thinking, and your fear of loneliness and resistance to change. Love and accept yourself for who you are and where you are. Stop denying what you want. Ask for help from your guides. Release resistance and trust that the universe will take you where you need to go.

Chapter 6
BELIEFS ABOUT INTUITION

As you walk your path, you may encounter information that sends you on a detour. Intellectually focused teachers or friends who insist their information is correct can send you down a blind alley if you listen to them over yourself. This chapter covers some commonly held beliefs and provides an alternate perspective on them.

As you read, please remember one caveat: There is no single truth. Each human is different and has a unique life experience, information, and perspective. There are no mistakes. You can travel far on a belief until you discard it and choose a different one. You only have to look at the placebo effect to see that. The best way to approach this chapter is to remain open, yet retain your own unique perspective. Please accept only what is correct for you. After all, this is my unique perspective at the time of writing. My beliefs change over time with new information and so do yours.

Keep all this in mind as you read the following beliefs about intuition, intuitive people, and ways of accessing intuitive information.

Belief: You Must Wait for Insights to Come to You

Sudden flashes of insight are how most untrained people experience intuition. This can be a once-in-a-lifetime occurrence that makes a great story at dinner or a more frequent event. Either way, most people believe they can't control intuition, so they wait for it to happen to them. There are well-respected professionals and famous mediums who believe this is how intuition works.

Beginners and experienced psychics alike do not always realize they can consciously access intuition at will. Yet by learning a few key principles, everyone can control their intuition. You can develop your intuition so you can tune in anytime you wish. Using the methods presented in Part Three, you can develop it to the degree that you can get information about whatever you want whenever you want. Flashes of insight may still occur, but you won't have to passively wait for it anymore. Once you can consciously work with your intuition, new possibilities open for you. From then on your inner guidance is at your fingertips.

Belief: You're Not Always Connected to Your Intuition

Your soul is always communicating with you through your higher consciousness. You are constantly connected to its information flow. It is the stream of consciousness that you are projected from. You are part of it. You may not always be consciously aware of it, however, as your physical senses, intellect, emotions, and other body aspects may dominate your consciousness instead. This is a necessary part of being in a physical body. How else could you navigate the physical world? But it can cause you to lose sight of your intuition.

Tuning out external influences can help you tune in to your internal world. This is why meditation and intuition development are intricately connected. Intuition works in different ways for different people. Understanding your unique intuitive style can help you connect and consciously work with it.

Belief: Intuition Is Always Clear

Some people believe they are not intuitive because their experiences of intuition have been vague and fleeting. In truth, intuition is subtle for most people who have not been trained to recognize it. It can be a cloudy image that momentarily flashes across your mental screen, or a faraway voice floating on the wind. It can be a gut feeling or a vague sense of knowing. If you are not practiced at using your intuition, your mind may be busy with many voices. Your mental screen might be overloaded with images from your day or the movie you just watched. Before you even recognize an insight, it's gone. Even if you do pick up the quiet voice of your intuition, you may analyze it through your logical mind and lose its essence.

Meditation can help you identify and develop your intuition. It helps you calm down and clears your mind so you can access intuition despite the veil of the intellect and physical senses. The more you focus on intuition, the clearer it becomes. It can be helpful to have a teacher to start. A mentor can teach you how to consciously access your intuition faster than you might figure out on your own. Plus, he or she can validate when you really are using your intuition.

Belief: Intuition Always Makes Sense

Intuition does not necessarily always make logical sense. Sometimes it can be in conflict with your mind. Let's say you meet a new guy and your intuition says, "Stay Away!" On the surface, he is charming, polite, and treats you well. He has a good job, a house, and says he is looking for commitment. Your logical mind would set you up with him in an instant. But what if there is something he isn't telling you? Maybe he is lying. Perhaps he is a criminal and you're in danger. Your intuition might be warning you through a strong gut instinct or inner knowing that this person is not for you.

Intuition doesn't work like a machine or a math problem. It is information emerging instantly without logic. Sometimes it brings a different message to your mind. But it is the voice of your higher being and offers trusted guidance. Of course, you have the choice to listen to logic or intuition. Either way, you will create new life experiences to learn from.

Belief: Intuition Can Be Wrong

Wrong! Your intuition is always right for you! Someone else's intuition could be wrong for you, and your intuition could be wrong for them. We don't always see things the same way, even when operating intuitively. But if you are tuning-in correctly, accepting the information as is and not passing it through your intellectual, emotional, or sexual filters, then it is giving you good guidance.

If you listen, trust, and act on your intuition, then it is always in your best interests. What's more, your intuition can help you see why this is a good idea and how even a seemingly painful choice is in your best interest. If you believe you followed your intuition and something turned out badly, then it may not have been your intuition.

Belief: Women Are Better at Intuition

There are more practicing female psychics than male. This relates more to social influences than a difference in ability. Women and men are born with the same gifts but receive different cultural programming. Society gives permission to women to practice "women's intuition." Men are given the message that they must be strong, rational, and realistic. This mental training makes men lose touch with their inner wisdom.

Even when we acknowledge intuition in both sexes, there are different stereotypes. Men have permission for gut feelings and business instincts. They can be visionaries or futurists. They can intuitively decode technology and find directions. Women can have women's intuition and a mother's instinct. Female intuition is mysterious, goddess-like, illogical, and to be feared. So while women have more permission to be intuitive, they can also be invalidated because of it.

Everyone has intuition. Whether you are male or female, one of the most valuable things you can do is to learn to receive and follow your intuition. Whether you want to use it in the boardroom, ballroom, or ballpark, intuition can support your life journey. As spirit, we are genderless. There is a frequency difference between female and male bodies, because of the energy it takes to conceive, gestate, and birth another person. This higher vibration can aid those in a female body to access their intuition.

Belief: Only Special People Have Intuition

Some psychics perpetuate a myth that they have special and mysterious gifts that are inaccessible to ordinary folk. They may say it runs in their family, they are the seventh son of a seventh son, have been initiated into a special group, or anointed as the chosen one in a long line of gifted gurus. Their argument is that people need to go to them for answers. Everyone is intuitive and can receive their answers directly from source. Of course, not everyone chooses an intuitive path. Some people are happy focusing on the physical experience. However, anyone who wants to can learn to access their intuition directly without giving their power away.

Belief: Psychics Are Evil

The words *psychic, medium, intuitive, gifted, sensitive, empathic*, and *extra sensory perception* are used for people with intuition. Each word comes with an energy charge depending on how it is being perceived and judged. Some religious factions perceive *psychic* to mean you are engaged in the work of the devil. *Medium* is more accepted as it is believed to mean that you are at least trying to help people by talking to dead relatives or solving a crime.

Sensitive and empathic people are perceived as emotionally unstable. Gifted people are special but abnormal outliers. Those with extra sensory perception perform black ops for the government.

If you are intuitive, you are gifted but not so much to be scary. I use the word *intuitive* as it seems less likely to cause affront, and yet describes what I do. People with intuition are not evil. They are conscious individuals who can perceive nonphysical reality. Because being intuitive is still taboo in many circles, some hide or avoid their gifts for fear of other's judgment and misperceptions.

Belief: The Labels Indigo, Rainbow, Crystal, and Starseed Children Apply to Different Generations

We have given labels to different generations depending on their collective purpose and perceived sensitivities. As a consequence, many people are confused about their identity. They wonder if they are really an alien from another planet, an angel, a fairy, or a new species of human.

While it is true that as spirit you create in many realities, the aspect of you that is in this body is human. Your unique spark of consciousness is meant to experience this reality. By focusing on aspects of yourself in other realities or the fantasy of not being human, you miss the opportunity this life presents. Humanity is evolving. Each generation learns and grows and paves the way for the next. Some of the new kids have parents who are more open to intuition so they don't receive the same limits as previous generations.

Our planet is at the forefront of the expansion of consciousness because of its density and polarity, and we are in a planetary cycle of rapid growth and change. So we are an attraction for all beings who want to experience rapid expansion. While there are individuals here in human bodies from other planets, they are now equally human. Being from a "more evolved world" doesn't mean it will be easy when you put on your human body and walk among the earthlings. We are all divine energy beings birthed from stars and source energy. Every single one of us can choose to access our intuition, regardless of the other realities we all create in.

Belief: The Power Is in the Object

The classic notion of a psychic is a gypsy who uses tarot cards, a crystal ball, or another ritual object to predict the future. This has given the impression that the power of intuition comes from the object, not the reader. Such objects can be great tools for stimulating intuition. Cards can help you bypass the intellect, as the images can stimulate the imagination. But if you memorize the manual that came with the cards, you are relying on your memory and intellect for meaning and not your intuition.

A skilled reader may use objects to help them focus, stimulate intuition, or draw the client's energy away enabling them to read more clearly. While it might appear that it's the object that is special, intuition is the genuine information source.

Belief: The Future Is Predetermined

Most people don't want to take responsibility for their lives. They certainly don't wish to hear that they create their reality as that means they are responsible for their past, present, and future life creations. They visit psychics to find out when they will meet their next lover, if they will be successful in their job interview, or when they will get that financial windfall they are counting on.

There are infinite possibilities projecting like branches from where you are now in time or space. Every possibility you want and don't want lies before you somewhere in this tree. The path you take is shaped by your consciousness. Any prediction of your future is based on the most likely probability given your current intentions, beliefs, and desires.

I rarely predict the future for people as I believe in free will and your ability to consciously create your preferred reality. On the rare occasion I do, I assign a likelihood to it. Predicting your future could disempower you, limit your creativity, or prevent you taking responsibility for your life.

Belief: The Third Eye is Solely Responsible for Intuition

There is a misconception that the sixth chakra governs all forms of intuition. This is not true. All your chakras are involved in spiritual communication, although working through your sixth chakra is unbelievably helpful for operating consciously as spirit in a body. The third eye is a powerful determinant of conscious awareness. Located in the pineal gland in the center of your sixth chakra, it helps you be neutral, be accepting, and have great clarity about yourself, others, and your life creations. Your sixth chakra is the channel for abstract intuition and clairvoyance. Sitting in your third eye helps you see energy, interpret symbols, and become aware of out-of-body beings.

However, as you have learned in this book, the other main chakras are also involved in spiritual communication. Your crown center helps you connect with your wisdom. The throat center channels your inner voice, telepathy, clairaudience, and pragmatic intuition. Your heart center guides you through the magnetic attraction of affinity and the interconnection of all things via the aspect of oneness. The solar plexus helps you channel your energy through creations on Earth and in other dimensions. Your sacral center confers emotional intuition. The root center connects you to your survival instinct.

There are many forms of intuition to explore. Your third eye gives you the neutrality you need to deal with what comes up as you use intuition to know yourself and others better.

Belief: Your Aura Is One Fixed Color

I am amused when someone asks me, "What color is my aura?" or tells me they were told their aura color years ago so they know what it is. They say things such as it is blue because I am a healer or orange meaning I am passionate. They may well have those tendencies, but the aura is not one color that you retain for life.

Your energy field is dynamic, multilayered, multicolored, and is always changing. Today, your first chakra might emanate red as you channel the life force needed to run a triathlon. Tomorrow, it might channel blue as it heals the body from the torn ligament and muscle strains from the day before. Last week, your heart chakra might run gold energy as you just had a new baby and are opening to the love of being a parent. Next week, it might run a green vibration as you learn how to take care of your new baby.

Belief: Chakras Must Be Specific Colors

You may have been taught that your chakras are certain colors. To be healthy, they should always be red (first), orange (second), yellow (third), green (fourth), blue (fifth), indigo (sixth), and violet (seventh). If they are not these colors, then something is wrong.

This system for teaching about chakras uses the rainbow colors that emerge when clear light is split by a prism to show the elevation in frequency as you move from the first to the seventh. The first, being associated with the material world has the lowest frequency. The crown, as the gateway to spirit, has the highest frequency.

Your chakras are a dynamic system. To my clairvoyant vision, the colors are always changing. You channel different energy frequencies through them as you respond to changing circumstances. From my personal experience, any chakra or layer of the auric field can appear to be any color. The colors reflect what is being experienced in your life now. I believe there is not one correct color for them, but many colors. These colors change as you face life challenges and process life experiences.

Belief: You Must Open Your Chakras

Some spiritual seekers believe that to become enlightened, you must open all your chakras. Opening a chakra is not the same as unsealing the wisdom it contains. Chakra mastery is more about being aware of your chakras and the information you stored in them, and the ability to modulate them to achieve the states of consciousness you wish. This comes with experience and observation of what happens when chakras are more open or closed or by following the guidance of a good teacher to help you avoid the pitfalls.

Here are some examples to help illustrate the point. If your crown chakra is narrowly opened, you can access all your information and channel source energy in a way that relates to you and your life. If it is wide open, you can access the entire universe and beyond, which includes information that makes no sense to people on this planet. If your throat chakra is narrowly opened, you can access your inner voice and tune out all the other voices. If it is more open, you will hear many signals from all manner of physical and nonphysical beings.

In a general sense, if your third chakra is more open, you will own your power. If it is more closed, you might be in fear and feeling disempowered. So the question is really, "What experience of reality do you wish to have?" You can modulate your chakras to accommodate it. If you want to enter a trance state to do intuitive readings, that requires a very different chakra configuration than if you want to play baseball or tennis.

Belief: Channeling Is the Highest Form of Intuition

Channeling is the ability to bring a spirit or entity through the physical body. When a medium channels another being, she is using trance-mediumship. She leaves her physical body and allows the entity to take possession. Famous channels include J. Z. Knight, who channeled Ramtha; Jane Roberts with Seth; Esther Hicks with Abraham; Darryl Anka with Bashar; and Edgar Cayce, the sleeping prophet, who was not present in his body when he gave his readings.

There are many degrees of channeling as well. Some mediums channel other aspects of themselves. Others share energy with a spirit without giving up complete control of their body. Lee Carroll channeling Kryon is an example of this.

All of these channels have brought us important information about our growth. The myth about channeling is that it is the best or only way to retrieve higher information. This isn't true because you can communicate with other beings without inviting them to take over your body.

Some people are attracted to channeling because they believe it will bring power, status, fame, and fortune. They attempt it without the proper preparation for the body or discernment regarding who they are allowing into their space. If you first choose to prepare your body through meditation, develop your own intuition and channel your higher self, you can make an informed decision about whether this is for you.

Belief: Mediumship Is a Specific Ability

People often think of mediumship as a specific skill in itself. While trance mediumship is the ability to channel spirit, many people we call mediums are actually using other intuitive abilities to access their information. A spiritual medium is a communication conduit between the spirit world and physical reality. Typically, they contact deceased loved ones or spirit guides; although in the popular TV series *The Medium*, the star was able to see remotely through dreams and visions.

There are many ways mediums receive messages. A friend training to be a medium uses her clairsentience, so she often says, "I am feeling..." Some mediums use clairvoyance and say, "I am seeing..." Others use their clairaudience, "I am hearing..." Still others "know" and are using knowingness. Some mediums use several psychic senses simultaneously to receive their messages. Some are not using psychic senses but are actually experiencing entities directly stimulating their physical senses.

Belief: Clairolfaction Is a Psychic Ability

Clairolfaction is perceived by some psychics to be an aspect of the first chakra, which governs the limbic system and deals with the physical sense of smell, survival, emotions, and long-term memory. Some spiritual mediums allow their sense of smell to be stimulated as a way to receive and communicate information. This actually isn't a true spiritual sense. In our noncorporeal form, we don't smell. Yet a medium smells cigars and deduces she is speaking to your grandfather, who loved cigars. You smell baking and assume Auntie Nellie, who always baked fresh bread, is visiting. As there is no physical source of the smell, spiritual smelling is assumed to be a genuine intuitive gift. So what is going on?

Spirit is stimulating the physical sense of smell. A true spiritual sense is not being accessed through one of your chakras. This imbalance in body spirit communication can cause issues because foreign energy is entering the energetic system of the medium. If she doesn't clear it out, it will impact her reality. If you experience a smell that will not go away, you might accuse a friend of smoking in your car, believe you stink, or become paranoid. You might even believe you are ill. Your doctor might look for a brain tumor, cyst, infection, seizures, stroke, head trauma, Alzheimer's, migraine, or epilepsy.

When no physical cause is found, they could surgically modify your olfactory bulbs or prescribe psychiatric drugs, when all you need to do is own your space through meditation.

Belief: Clairgustance Is a Psychic Ability

Some mediums allow their taste buds to be stimulated to communicate information. For instance, a healer might taste herbs or a special diet for a patient. The information is seemingly coming through the taste buds, even though there is no physical substance on the tongue or in the mouth. Because the second chakra governs taste and emotions, some psychics claim clairgustance is an ability of that chakra. Instead, spirit is stimulating the sense of taste. You are not accessing a spiritual sense via a chakra.

If you unconsciously allow spirit to interfere by stimulating unreal tastes you might seek medical help. Conditions that can cause a "bad taste" are zinc deficiency, constipation, menopause, side effects to hypertension drugs, chemotherapy, and pesticide and heavy metal poisoning. In fact, some people diagnosed as schizophrenics have taste hallucinations and can't distinguish real from phantom tastes. I believe it is possible to be diagnosed with a mental illness or develop depression or an eating disorder when what is actually happening is a miscommunication between body and spirit.

Belief: Clairsentience Is a Sense of Touch

A man feels pressure in his chest. He later discovers a loved one had a heart attack. A spirit guide touches the top of a woman's head to let their presence be felt. A medium feels symptoms of an illness and uses it to identify who she is communicating with. A boy has a bad feeling; the next day he is in an accident.

I have heard all of the above be referred to as experiences of clairsentience. None of them really are and here is why. Clairsentience relates to the emotions and its purpose is body-spirit communication. Some people believe it includes physical sensations. However, when a physical sensation is felt, spirit can be stimulating the sense of physical touch.

The man is experiencing his loved one's reality because they are in each other's energy field. The being has invasively attached to the woman's crown chakra. Spirit has entered the medium's space and she is partially channeling this being. The boy is having a premonition.

This is not to say that you cannot feel the energy. You can feel the energy with your hand chakras. You can sense energy entering, leaving, and flowing through your energy field. The more you use your intuition to know and heal your space, the more sensitive you become to your energy, foreign energy, and energy shifts. I have also heard clairsentience called *clairtangency*. This term means clear touching and is another word for *psychometry*. Since childhood, I touched things using my invisible hands. I later came to call them my psychic healing hands. Eventually, I realized they are the hands in my astral body, which is another way you might feel energy intuitively.

Belief: Spirits Have Emotions

Some intuitive readers attribute emotions as belonging to spirit guides and deceased loved ones. Deceased Auntie Mary is angry because you married the wrong husband or Chief Wakanaka is disappointed you didn't take his advice. Disembodied beings do not have emotions. Only bodies have emotions. Once you die you no longer experience lower-vibration human emotions, though you do experience the higher vibrations such as love.

So when a medium perceives she feels an emotion from a spirit, it's because the being has entered her energy field and has stimulated her emotions. This could happen if the deceased wants to express how they were feeling when they died but do not yet know how to communicate respectfully as spirit. Or perhaps a malevolent spirit is deliberately being disruptive and manipulative. It could even be that the medium is not neutral and is projecting her emotionality onto the reading.

Belief: Synesthesia Is a Psychic Ability

Synesthesia is a medical condition where one sense is muddled with another, such as being able to smell or taste what you see and hear. A synesthetic person might read a recipe and taste what they see. Or they may watch television and smell what's in a show although it isn't physically present. I have heard it implied that having synesthesia makes you psychic. Yet this is a neurological phenomenon where stimulation of one sensory or cognitive pathway leads to automatic, involuntary experiences in a second sensory or cognitive pathway. While we do make spiritual communications conscious and relevant to our reality by translating them using the brain, they do not need to be scrambled through multiple neural pathways. The idea of an apple could be intuited by knowing it, seeing it as a vision, or hearing spirit say "apple." If you taste and smell an apple when you see it, that may result in a richer experience of apple, but this is not necessarily an experience of intuition.

IDENTIFY YOUR INTUITION BELIEFS EXERCISE

Take a moment to reflect on this chapter and make some notes on what you learned. List all of the beliefs about intuition that were busted for you. Next to them, write down whom or where the belief came from. Notice if there are specific people who have impacted you; these are some of your key influencers. You will work with them in Part Three.

Also make a note of when your information differed from mine. Give yourself permission to be unique, operate from free will, and access your own information.

Chapter 7
WHY DEVELOP INTUITION?

Inviting intuition into your life brings many benefits. It can help you:

- Have greater clarity.
- Feel more confident.
- Banish stress and anxiety.
- Be free to help yourself and others.
- Fearlessly trust your intuitive messages.
- Experience increased peace and happiness.
- Know how to tap into your intuition when you wish.
- Be guided by your higher self for better life decisions.

So take a leap of faith and invite intuition to play a bigger role in your life. Commit to following your higher guidance, and reap the rewards for the rest of your life. You can trust your intuition completely. Whether you struggle with a relationship, need to make a career change, are thinking of moving, or need to make important financial decisions, it always has your best interests at heart.

Intuition can teach you to have faith in yourself and your information versus giving your power away to the authority of others. The more you let yourself have and use your intuition the more you can cultivate well-being and trust in yourself, your capabilities, and guidance. It helps you take a higher perspective on life and gives you confidence in making your own decisions regardless of the desires and opinions of others.

Intuition transcends the intellect. It provides information in an instant, compared to logic, which weighs the pros and cons and leads from one idea to the next via linear thinking. The intellect can be the hardest body level to tame. If you have strong training in logic, you might pass your intuitive signals through your mind and analyze them until you lose sight of the original message. Intuition helps you draw from a broader scope of experience and open your mind to wider possibilities rather than be limited by cultural programming.

The more you listen to your intuition, the less internal conflict there is. Intuition helps you rise above your emotions. The aspects of the ego (such as greed, selfishness, the need to accumulate or dominate, self-hatred, self-judgment, and feelings of worthlessness) cease to drive your personality. Instead, you can reflect and act on your true feelings and desires; leading to peace and calm. Intuition also helps you tune in to your body so you can take better care of it. This leads to greater emotional satisfaction.

Listening to your intuition gives you awareness of your life purpose. Your gentle inner voice can lead you on a path of healing and growth by helping you let go of expectations and past experiences. So they cease to cloud your decisions and judgment. Your clairsentience helps you work with your body. Your clairvoyance gives you clarity. Your knowingness increases your certainty. Using your gifts opens a path to a happier, more insightful and better fulfilled you.

Intuition is Spiritual Communication

Intuition is spiritual communication and is an expression of love. When it is embraced and allowed, energy flows. When energy flows there is change, healing, and expansion. To withhold the flow of intuition is to lower your frequency, invite limitation, and prevent evolvement. You are an eternal spiritual being and your intuition helps you, the temporal self, to commune with you, the greater all-encompassing self.

Intuition is how we communicate as spirit. There are different ways of doing this and Part Two will explain them in detail. Each style of intuitive communication is uniquely valuable and confers specific advantages. You can emphasize and develop the ones that benefit you most, depending on your focus this lifetime. In the meantime, below are ten types of communication that intuition brings.

1. Divine

You are a part of the oneness of all creation. Some people call this God, but there are many other names used to describe it, including Supreme Being, Cosmic Consciousness, Trusted Source, and The Great All That Is. Wherever you see any of these terms mentioned in this book, feel free to substitute your preferred word to describe a higher power.

Your intuition enables you to commune with and receive information from your personal God, through your own concept of what God is. As God is all things, this means you have access to all knowledge, unless you have a limited concept of God. You are connected with everything that ever was, is, and ever will be in all places throughout creation. All can be known by you from your unique perspective through intuition.

2. Your Soul and Higher Self

You are so much more than your physical body. You are a multidimensional being of love and light that creates in multiple realities. Names for the greater aspects of your consciousness are spirit, soul, over-soul, and higher self. Your wisdom is vast and beyond logic. Your intuition helps you to know your own answers and receive your information from your unique perspective. It can be a great guiding force in your life. You can access whatever you need to know to assist you on your life journey at any time, any place, anywhere.

3. Multidimensional Self

Imagine what it would be like if you could tell a past version of you that everything was going to be alright. Or ask a future version of you to suggest the most joyful and expedient path to the desired outcome. If you wish, you can use your intuition to visit your past lives, ask what they learned from their Earthly experiences, and claim their skills and abilities to use in your life.

4. Angels and Guides

Everyone wonders about angels, guides, and ascended masters and wants to receive their guidance. They are always available to you. With your intuition, you will be able to see, hear, and feel them and know they are indeed present. You can consult them in your daytime experiences on the Earth plane, and travel with them in your nighttime adventures through the astral plane and other realities.

5. Dearly Departed

Perhaps your main reason for developing your intuition is because you want to connect with your loved ones after they pass. Your cherished partner and parents are not within reach through your physical senses, but they can be contacted when you use your intuition. Or maybe you want to investigate paranormal phenomena, and spending the night in a haunted house is your greatest ambition. If you develop your intuition, you will be able to detect the ghostly goings-on.

6. Other People

I am sure you have felt frustrated when you can't get through to someone no matter how hard you try. As spirit, we don't communicate through verbal language and body cues, we communicate through intuition. You can use your intuition to speak to people as spirit instead of the usual physical communication process. Sometimes this works much better as it can bypass their resistance and blocks. You can also tell when you are being lied to and see through people's facades.

7. Plants and Animals

Animals and plants communicate through a type of intuition. If you want your plants to grow faster, to understand why they are stunted, or find out where they should be planted to thrive, then your intuition can help you tune in to what is going on. Instead of projecting human characteristics onto your pets, you would be able to tune in to them directly and know how they are doing and what they need from you to be happy. You could also check in with pets who are sick to find out what they need, and speak to the ones who have passed.

8. Nature Spirits

Your intuition can also open you up to the Devic kingdom. These are the nature spirits that watch over all forms of nature, including mountains, waterfalls, forests, meadows, volcanoes and more. They are wonderful helper beings in service to our planet and focused on the ecology of the natural world. Every plant and tree has a nature spirit who watches over it and tends to its needs. They go by many different names. Some examples are fairies, elves, and dryads. Earth is a living being and you can also communicate with the spirit of Mother Earth using your intuition.

9. Body

You are not your physical body. You are the spirit that created it. Yet the body does have an innate consciousness. You can develop your intuition in a way that will allow you to listen to its needs to ensure it has what it requires for health and vitality. For instance, your intuition will tell you what to eat for more energy or to heal a physical issue. It can help you understand why your body is depressed or afraid and more.

10. Galactic Beings

We are not living on the only inhabited planet. There are many highly evolved groups of benevolent beings who are available to share their wisdom and assist us in our growth. Some of them look at us as though we were their children and grandchildren. They have been through what we are going through and know what works and what doesn't. Communicating with star beings can be an amazing experience and can help you with your spiritual growth. Some of these beings are from other dimensions and realities. Some are from higher dimensions and act as guides and teachers.

YOUR INTUITION WHY EXERCISE

Intuition is your spiritual communication system. It can help with everything and it's meant to be as much a part of your life as your physical senses. Your intuition allows you to connect with your personal God, your higher self, your body, other bodies, and more. You can rise above physical concerns and take a spiritual perspective. You can choose to listen to your intuition versus your intellect, emotions, or ego. Yet, what are your unique reasons for tuning in to your intuition? If you are not sure, spend some time now to get clearer.

Pick up your notebook and write about your reasons for wanting to develop your intuition. For instance, write about what intuition benefits excite you most, with whom you wish to communicate, and what you most want to use your intuition for.

There are many possibilities for whom you can connect with using your intuition. It's good to know who you want to talk to and why so that you can be discerning and focus your intention on that. Just as there are all sorts of humans, there are many beings more than willing to talk to you, although you might not want to talk to all of them. Some are benevolent and of a high vibration, others are not in alignment with source. Review the ten types of communication above and decide which ones most resonate with you. Find out whether you most want to develop your intuition to talk to your personal God and higher self, your guides, pets, friends, family, aliens, or spirits.

Also reflect on how you want to use your abilities. Are you mostly interested in being a medium, psychic, or spiritual counselor? Or do you wish to develop your full potential in your chosen field? I know doctors, lawyers, office workers, translators, realtors, nurses, environmental stewards, and CEOs who developed their intuition so they can focus on their path and make a difference. List what excites you about developing your intuition. Then go one step further and visualize how you want to apply it in your life. Let your passion and excitement flow.

Holding the frequency of excitement while visualizing what you want is part of the formula to consciously create your reality. It's like ordering a pizza. The universe is your pizza delivery guy and he always brings what you order. The frequency you vibrate at determines what you get so you don't get anchovies on your pizza when you prefer olives.

YOUR INTUITION WHERE EXERCISE

Once you know why you want to develop your intuition and who you want to interact with, you can now figure out where you are on the intuition development path. If you are early on in the path, you may be having the occasional awareness that happens randomly. Or you might be having dreams that are relevant to your earthly life. As you progress along the path, you can connect at will versus having random occurrences, and everything is much clearer, more obvious, and less fuzzy. Eventually, you will operate it at will, turn it on and off if you wish, as well as decide what to tune in to and what not to tune in to, so that you can confidently use it to help others.

Take stock of where you are now with your intuition. Ask the following questions and make notes in your notebook as you go along:

- How and when do I currently use my intuition?
- When don't I use it, and if not, why not?
- When I am aware of my intuition, do I always follow it?
- If I am ignoring my intuition, why am I doing so?
- Where is my energy going if not serving my passion?

Consider your daily life: your home, job, family, friends, health, fitness, finances, and other personal goals as well. I meet lots of people who can tune in to their intuition and follow its guidance, but who still wish to improve. If this is you, rest assured your goals are within reach.

The exercises in this book will help you, but finding a good teacher is essential; someone who has been where you are and can prevent you from stumbling along blindly. When you are very clear on why you want to develop your intuition, we can delve deeper into the mystery of spiritual communication.

Part Two

IDENTIFY YOUR INTUITION STYLE

Chapter 8
INTUITION AND THE
SEVENTH CHAKRA

This chapter provides an explanation of the intuitive information flowing through the seventh chakra, also known as the crown chakra and Sahasrara. This energy center is located on the top of your head. It connects you with higher frequencies and dimensions of reality. Your consciousness enters your body through the seventh chakra. It has information on how to channel yourself or others, and links to source energy and your higher wisdom. Seniority with this chakra lets you channel yourself and access information that relates to your current reality. When it is unbalanced, you may operate from information that isn't appropriate for you or that doesn't make sense in present time, or you might impose your perspective inappropriately on others. Used correctly it channels your ability to know everything you need to know to fulfill your purpose, and to bring your energy into the body so that you can make the most of your Earth journey.

The spiritual abilities covered in this chapter are trance mediumship and knowingness (claircognizance).

Trance Mediumship

Trance mediumship is the ability to bring spiritual energy into the physical body. Everyone alive on Earth is a trance medium. You are spirit, you have a body, and you have the ability to bring your spiritual consciousness into your body. We are all spiritual beings and have created our bodies to experience physical reality. Spirit exists outside of time and space. You, the eternal being, can be anytime, anyplace, anywhere. Your body can only be in the moment. Trance mediumship helps you, the high-vibration entity, connect with your body right here, right now. If you wish to consciously guide your life, it helps to gain control of this ability. If you are not present in your body, you can't possibly be in charge and your ego, pain, emotions, and intellect will dominate.

Trance mediumship can be used to channel you, divine source, or another entity. A challenge in gaining seniority with this ability is losing control of your own body. You could channel a trusted guide or be hijacked by a spirit against your will. In both cases, another being controls your body. While channeling and possession are extreme examples, we have all channeled someone else. If you have ever behaved out of character, perhaps like your Mum, Dad, or partner, you could have been channeling some of their energy through your body.

Conversely, if it is easy for you to get others to do and say what you want, you could be using trance mediumship to invade their space. This treasured gift is meant to give you access to your personal space so you can create through it. You are the god of your own universe and are capable of taking charge of it. If you want to consciously create a purpose-filled life, your trance mediumship can help you because it gives you access to physical reality through your body.

My First Experiences Channeling a Guide

Over twenty years ago, I took my first formal training as a healer with one of the United Kingdom's leading energy healers. The course focused on sensing and working with the energy field and chakras, as well as with healing guides. It was amazing to experience energy in this way and be validated for my experiences. My spirit guide at the time was a deceased doctor. When we conducted a healing together, he stepped into my body and operated my arms and legs. He moved me into various stances and channeled healing energy through my arms and out my hands to assist the people we were working on. I loved every minute as it was my first significant experience of working with a healing guide.

A few years later, I joined a program for healers and psychics taught by Mary Ellen Flora. I couldn't contain my excitement as I drove to my first session. I traveled with one of my guides sitting in my body chatting about the scenery all the way there. I thought the way I worked with guides was natural. Imagine my shock when we finally started learning about them. We were taught to be senior to guides, to talk to them using our intuition without allowing them to take over the body.

My teacher explained that the high energy of the guide could be harmful if the body wasn't properly prepared. Since then I don't work with guides who want to use my body. Instead, I channel my own higher consciousness and communicate with guides using my intuition. I know, hear, and communicate telepathically with my guides. Allowing them to use my body is not necessary. Instead, we have a conversation; although I do allow my current healing guides to connect with my energy in a respectful way on my invitation.

Nowadays, I use my trance mediumship when I am doing a reading. I arrange my chakras in a specific energy configuration to enter a trance state. This altered state of consciousness helps me tune out the physical world and tune in to the nonphysical world. My trance mediumship allows me to consciously make shifts in energy frequencies at my crown chakra so that I become aware of and deliver accurate and relevant information to the person I am talking to. It also helps me write, paint, and be creative.

Discovering Your Trance Mediumship

Every human is a trance medium. You are spirit and you have a body. Your trance mediumship helps you be present within the body and own your space. By taking charge of your trance mediumship, you channel yourself. Not being in charge of your trance mediumship can leave you vulnerable to other energies taking over, also known as possession. Occasionally, a person has a spiritual contract with a high-vibration being to deliver teachings by channeling it, an example being Lee Carroll and Kryon. It is also possible to channel higher aspects of your own being, as is the case with Esther Hicks and Abraham.

Being able to channel a light being and bring through teachings for humanity sounds amazing. It took Esther Hicks a year of focused meditation to begin to channel Abraham. I spent many years in a modern-day mystery school, where I cleared my energy so that I could consciously channel my higher self and modulate my energies and chakras at will. We all start somewhere. Below are some common experiences to help you identify when and how your trance mediumship has already been at play in your life.

If you feel disconnected from your body, or uncomfortable in your own skin, you likely don't have seniority with your trance mediumship. If you don't know why you say or do things, behave out of character, or seem to have multiple personalities, you may be channeling entities. If you have ever found yourself saying or doing something like someone else you know, you may be channeling them. If you are a different person when you consume drugs or alcohol, you may be leaving your body as a result of the altered state of consciousness and channeling another being. It is tempting to escape your pain, whether by sleeping, watching TV, or getting drunk. If your life feels out of control, the way to counteract this is to get into your body. If you are absent, you leave the body vulnerable to other energies and will find it difficult to get back on track and create the life you want.

Most people do not fully channel their consciousness through their body as they are meant to. Our culture isn't set up to support this. Take, for example, a bored kid at school or an office worker at a tedious meeting. It can be tempting to drift off, but when this happens you disassociate from the body and physical reality. An awakened human is grounded and uses their trance mediumship to be present, awake, and aware.

A different challenge of trance mediumship relates to using it to control others. If it is easy for you to get others to do and say what you want, or if your presence in a room makes others feel unsafe, and go quiet, your trance mediumship may be out of control. You may be unconsciously influencing the reality of others and invading their space. Even if you haven't done this, I am sure you have experienced situations like it and heard about it on the news. David Koresh[17] and the siege in Waco, Texas, and Jim Jones,[18] who incited a mass suicide in Jonestown, are both examples of out-of-control trance mediums.

---

17. Wikipedia contributors. David Koresh. Wikipedia, The Free Encyclopedia. https://en.wikipedia.org/w/index.php?title=David_Koresh&oldid=894411703. Accessed April 30, 2019.

18. Wikipedia contributors. Jim Jones. Wikipedia, The Free Encyclopedia. https://en.wikipedia.org/w/index.php?title=Jim_Jones&oldid=894209127. Accessed April 30, 2019.

I'll never forget a lunch I attended where the speaker was a powerful world leader. It was at a biotechnology conference, but he talked about terrorism. Every time he said we are going to kill the terrorists, we all stood up and applauded. There were thousands of people present, less than half from his country. We entered a mass trance. Afterwards, people shook their heads and talked about how they didn't even agree with the speaker. This is an extreme example that illustrates the power of trance mediumship. We are each responsible to take charge of our own energy. Below is a story about someone who did just that.

When Eddie Learned to Own His Space

Eddie was struggling to create the life he wanted. He didn't have a job and felt powerless. Initially, he came to me for readings and clarity on why he had created these difficulties. Eddie wanted to take charge of his life so I taught him techniques to help him come more into his body and take control. As he focused on using his trance mediumship to own his body and his intuitive abilities, he became calmer and started to believe in himself again.

Eddie had to focus on releasing energy he had stored in his body from past experiences and other people. The more he cleared out this foreign energy, the more of his own energy he could hold and the more he became himself. His family, who came from a culture that believed in curses, had no ethics about using their trance mediumship to control him.

With the use of the techniques in this book, Eddie started to take charge and his life turned around. He found a job he liked, started a new relationship, and gained seniority with his life. As he came more and more into his body, we started to discover what a powerful healer and intuitive he was. One day in a second-hand bookstore, he found an old book that contained spiritual teachings he had known in a past life. His trance mediumship helped him bring the prior knowledge into his body. His knowingness helped him access deeper meaning in these teachings so he could adapt them for present-day use.

Knowingness

Knowingness, or claircognizance (meaning clear knowing), is the ability to simply be still and know yourself, your spiritual information, and information relevant to your everyday life. If you have ever experienced inexplicable certainty, then you have experienced this ability. I am sure you have heard stories of people who knew not to take a flight, and later discovered it had crashed or been diverted, or who knew to take a different route to work, only to discover there was an accident on their usual route. In these cases, the receiver of the information can't explain logically how they knew; they just did.

Another common experience is to get a feeling about a new person who comes into your life. By all appearances, he looks like a nice guy, but you know not to get involved romantically; or a woman seems legitimate, but you know not to do business with her. Then later you discover he was married or she was a crook and so it was good you didn't date him or do business with her. If you ever misplaced something then knew where it was, it could be your claircognizance that found it. In fact, it's one of the most commonly recognized intuitive abilities. If you instantly receive clear and accurate information that you act on without analyzing it, or if you say things such as, "I'll know it when I see it," you are using this type of intuition.

Claircognizance refers to your ability to tune in to your divine wisdom. It allows you to enter a state of stillness where you can instantly know your spiritual information. When you use your knowingness, you clearly know without needing any supporting, external information, logic, or reason. You just know it without a shadow of a doubt. Your brain is more limited than your knowingness. It stores information just from your current lifetime like a computer. However, a broader repository of eternal wisdom can be accessed using your knowingness. It may help if you can perceive yourself as a stream of eternal consciousness. You might have had thousands of bodies and millennia of learning on Earth and in other realities. Everything you learned from them is available to you now through your knowingness. If you know things, when there's no rhyme or reason for it, no logic, no information you can point to, you too are using your knowingness.

How I Learned to Trust My Knowing

I use my knowingness a lot when I am teaching. It helps me access my higher information instantly, answer questions without thinking, and know what is going on with students. It also kicks in when I am being lied to.

This caused me grief before I validated my intuition, especially at work. The biotechnology industry is volatile. Most companies operate on investors' capital to develop their ideas. Most drugs don't make it to market and the companies are constantly restructuring and reinventing themselves. This doesn't allow for a secure work environment. Departments close, resources are reassigned, and people are let go. I went through three downsizings and seven mergers during my past career. If my position or department was under discussion, I could sense it. On the surface all was well, but simmering beneath was an evil plan. It makes for a very paranoid existence when outer reality doesn't match what you know inside.

I believe most humans live in a double reality like this, where the projected truth and the underlying truth are different—whether it's your friend telling you she likes your dress when she really thinks it is hideous, your boss wishing you a happy holiday while he squirms inside because he knows you will be laid off when you return, or a world leader making a declaration of war based on false evidence. Looking back on my career, had I been less fearful, I could have validated my knowing, let go of judgment, and accepted people and situations as they were. Then I might have been able to let go of resistance and plan ahead. I did meditate and it helped me cope, but the duplicity outraged me and at the time I felt powerless against it.

Discovering Your Sense of Knowing

You definitely have a sense of knowing. You are an infinite spirit and are very experienced and wise. The trick is how to access this wisdom, and one of the ways is through claircognizance. Let's explore how this form of intuition may have already impacted your life.

If you were constantly asking questions in childhood and were your family's little know-it-all, this is an early sign you were using your claircognizance. This may have been amusing and annoying to the adults around you, especially if you knew things they'd rather you didn't. They might have redirected your focus, told you to be quiet, and shut you down. As a consequence, the adult version of you could have issues with authority and feel controlled by others. You might also feel invalidated and unworthy because when you let your light shine as a child, it wasn't appreciated.

If you were lucky not to have been invalidated as a child, then your clair-cognizance could make you open-minded to new ideas. You could have faith in your higher self or a divine consciousness that directs your life. You might rely on your inner knowing more than your intellect, and relish a challenge because you always know your way out of it. Other signs that claircognizance is active in your life include knowing about something without knowing how, being able to easily discern when people are lying, and when you meet someone new, automatically knowing what kind of person they are.

Sometimes, when the crown chakra is going through a spiritual opening, it's possible to go out of bounds with your knowing. You can know things that aren't relevant to this time-space reality. David Icke is an example of a public figure who went through this type of experience. He was a sports presenter who had a spiritual opening and was indiscriminate about the information he shared. He became a conspiracy theorist, and said the British Royal Family were shape shifting lizards, and the moon was a mind control device. He was called crazy and ridiculed for many years as a result.

This is usually what happens when people get a Messiah complex. They start to access the vast field of knowledge and believe they must be special, their truth applies to everyone, and it is imperative they spread the word. We are all special and everyone can access all knowledge they need to guide their life journey through their own knowingness. Each of us has a unique per-spective. No single one of us has all the answers, although our perspectives might overlap. This is why David Icke's information makes sense to some people, but not to others.

When you become aware of how much you know, it can be difficult to stand back and let others figure things out on their own. If decision mak-ing is easy for you, meaning you always know what to do, you might find it frustrating when others dither. Or you may feel they should take you at your word and follow your direction. A superiority complex is just the ego hijack-ing the show. Each human is unique and has a unique perspective. No two individuals travel the same path. This means that your perspective and stage of growth is just as valid as another's. When we accept ourselves and others as we are, we allow everyone the space to keep growing.

Nellie Mastered Knowing By Not Competing

Nellie is very focused on her spiritual growth and used to be part of a psychic development circle. Yet when she came to me she was feeling blocked and felt that the others in her group were progressing faster than she was. Most were able to see spiritual phenomena using their clairvoyance, and some of them could feel things through their clairsentience. Nellie's most prevalent ability was knowingness, but she was having trouble acting on or speaking what she knew. She invalidated her information because she compared herself to her teacher and others in the group who were seeing and feeling their information. Nellie gave her power away in favor of the information that others received as well as believing that the way they got their intuitive information was better. She believed her insights were wrong because her experience was different from theirs.

I helped Nellie by teaching her to meditate. As she turned within, released foreign energy, and focused on her information, she could easily recognize and validate her higher wisdom. We also did work to help clear past experiences where others had not listened to her or had invalidated her information. The more she cleared the past, the more she owned her information in the present and was less concerned with being different.

Chapter 9

INTUITION AND THE SIXTH CHAKRA

This chapter provides an explanation of the intuitive information flowing through the sixth chakra, which is also known as the brow chakra, third eye, or Ajna. This energy center is located in the center of your forehead. It allows you to tune in to nonphysical reality, see the energy of spirit, and observe light beings and energy frequencies, such as electro-magnetic energy in the auric fields of people, plants, animals, and objects. It helps you see your truth in a clear light and validate what is real. You can use it to communicate with your higher self, source energy, and other beings.

Your sixth chakra channels information on abilities that let you perceive colors, shapes, vibrations, and energy frequencies in this reality and multidimensionally. It helps you see what is with neutrality, clarity, and acceptance. When you don't own your sixth chakra, you can lack clarity or be drawn into mental, emotional, or physical dramas. You may lack your own perspective and be fooled into seeing things through the eyes of others. Sometimes we avoid seeing our truth because we want to pretend everything is alright when it isn't or we are not ready to change. Your clairvoyance helps you discover and validate your own truth, and communicate through the language of light and frequency. Your abstract intuition helps you translate the formulas and symbols into meaning.

For me, these are my superhero powers. Imagine seeing into a person's physical body like a human CAT scanner or observing their aura and chakras for healing purposes. Imagine looking at your past lives, subpersonalities, and guides. It is better than any movie or TV show and is available for you to develop. Whether you use it to help others, for yourself, or to see this reality or other realities is your choice.

The spiritual abilities covered in this chapter are Clairvoyance, Abstract Intuition, and Precognition.

Clairvoyance

Clairvoyance is the ability to see clearly. It includes seeing nonphysical beings such as spirit guides, angels, ascended masters, saints, deceased loved ones, and ghosts, as well as energy vibrations, auras, chakras, pictures, and symbols. Remote viewing is a specific type of clairvoyance, where the viewer seeks impressions about a distant and unseen person, object, or target, usually in real time, or to see a past event. The most common time people begin to experience their clairvoyance is before sleeping, on waking, or during meditation, as much else can distract you during the day. Below are some signs that you're starting to experience clairvoyance:

- colors (energy vibrations) behind your forehead
- faces coming and going as you drop off to sleep
- fleeting visions remaining with you on waking
- waking visions of deceased loved ones or guides
- easily visualizing a relaxing scene during meditation
- remembering texts you have read visually
- seeing memories in your mind's eye

The intellect is the main block in developing clairvoyance. Most people are trained to focus on their intellect from an early age. Unfortunately, it slows down the flow of intuitive signals or causes people to ignore them entirely. By developing your clairvoyance, you can see clearly about yourself, those around you, and the situations you are in. You can take an intuitive perspective rather than a physical one. You see clearly regardless of the ego's projections.

Your clairvoyance gives you the neutrality you need to let go of your limits. It can help you get clear about how someone else's beliefs are influencing you, as well as being neutral and nonjudgmental about what you see. Electromagnetic energy waves are visible to a clairvoyant as color vibrations. The human energy field or aura is seen as color. Color has meaning and can be translated into language. Experiences, beliefs, and attitudes are also recorded in the energy field. These units of structured energy are visible to a clairvoyant as symbols, pictures, formulas, and vignettes. They contain much information that can be understood and translated.

My First Experiences Seeing Energy

I have always seen spiritual phenomena. For me, the world is alive with vibrant energy in motion. As a child, I saw multicolored lights blinking against the backdrop of darkness in my room at night. During the day, I see lights in the sky and trees. At first when I realized other people didn't see what I saw it didn't bother me too much. I shrugged my shoulders and adapted to the world as they saw it, but there were times when I questioned my sanity.

I left home for the first time to do a one-year work placement while I was studying to earn my bachelor's degree. I was twenty years old and shared a house with three other people. I remember sitting in the living room looking at the furniture, clearly seeing that it was not real. I was in a kind of virtual reality. Objects were not solid and I could make the furniture appear to float. In my mind, I repeated, "This chair isn't real, this table isn't real." I could see it wasn't. This was before home computers, the Matrix movies, or virtual reality computer games, and I wasn't on drugs. I had a choice: pull myself together or spiral into what I thought must be madness. I chose the former. Imagine my surprise years later, when I read the opening pages of *A Course in Miracles*. The first teaching is to appreciate that everything you see is not real. Or when I read *Seth Dreams and Projections of Consciousness* by Jane Roberts about how reality is a projection of our consciousness.

Nowadays, I do not question my clairvoyance. It is my strongest ability and I can flip between nonphysical and physical reality instantly or see both simultaneously. I see energy, auras, chakras, and guides, and I spend my days using my gift to help others.[19] One of the most profound experiences I

---

19. https://drlesleyphillips.com/readings/

had since validating my ability was actually seeing nothing. I was on a hike through Othello Tunnels near Hope, British Columbia, Canada. There was a group of hikers and I had buddied up with two fast-walking strangers. We were in the midst of a tunnel side by side when suddenly everything disappeared. We were suspended in space. Energy rushed past us—under our feet, over our heads, and all around. It felt like we were being shot through space.

At first, I didn't say anything, thinking it was just me and my psychic abilities, but when both women shrieked I realized it was a shared experience. We couldn't believe what was happening. We still had our bodies but nothing else existed besides the speeding energy. We reached the tunnel exit and normal reality resumed. Retracing our steps did not re-create the experience. We waited for the other hikers, and when they arrived they reported that their hike was ordinary. Once the hike was over, I never saw those women again. We had created the experience together to validate we are spirit and there is more to this reality than meets the physical eyes.

It's common for people to doubt their intuition when it doesn't match preconceived ideas of reality, or to invalidate it for fear of being accused of madness. But if you can accept and embrace it, life becomes even more vibrant and rich.

Discovering Your Clairvoyance

Clairvoyance can be difficult for people to validate, because they doubt it and think it's just their imagination. Or they expect it to be crystal clear and so if the images are not as clear as with their eyesight they don't believe they are doing it right. Usually, all it takes is to have an experienced clairvoyant validate you are having genuine experiences and give guidance on how to best harness your gift. These are clues that you are already using your clairvoyance, even though you might not have been calling it that.

We can use clairvoyance to recall past events, people, and objects as images. Though we might call this memory, not everyone recalls memories as images. We can use it to picture future plans in our minds. We call this visualization, but it is essentially the same as clairvoyance. We are projecting a thought form onto a visual image screen in both cases. If you picture someone you are having a phone conversation with in your mind's eye or see the characters in your imagination when you read a book, you are using your clairvoyance to have a multisensory experience.

I once had a boss who asked me if I had a photographic memory. I was stumped at the time because it was before I took training in clairvoyance, but when I look back now this was a sign that I didn't see things the same way others did. Other early clues that you might identify with are having an invisible friend as a child; seeing colors or faces when you go to sleep; or noticing colors around people, animals, plants, or inanimate objects.

Other signs of clairvoyance include using commonly used phrases such as "seeing red," "feeling blue," or "cowardly custard," or if colors affect your mood and you can read people by the colors they wear. Of course, if you have ever seen a ghost, had a vision of someone who was dead, or seen incidents from other people's lives that they did not tell you about, these are all big clues that your clairvoyance was at play.

Christina Overcomes Self-Doubt

Christina is an engineer with an interest in intuition, yoga, and hypnotherapy. She had some unexplained, intuitive experiences and wanted to learn more about them. I mentored Christina using a framework of tools so she could consciously access her intuition. She was a gifted clairvoyant who quickly learned to use her sixth chakra. Despite the fact that she was able to follow my guidance and see images using her clairvoyance, she remained blocked by her intense self-doubt. Christina was always questioning whether her faculties were real and needed lots of encouragement and support. She also needed help to let go of past experiences where people put her down. It took time, but now Christina does believe she is intuitive and is freeing herself from limits to using it. She loves her intuition and now uses her inner guidance for life decisions. While she doesn't want to be a full-time intuitive, she is planning on studying energy medicine and using her clairvoyance to see the energetic reality of people she assists.

Abstract Intuition

Humans have learned to communicate through language, be it verbal, sign, or body language. Spirit communicates using light, symbols, formulae, geometry, equations, and other vibrations, which convey more information than language ever could. Plus, they can be understood via the sixth chakra without using the intellect. If you knew the answer to questions in math class without having to work them out, you might have been using your abstract intuition. This is the ability of child prodigies,[20] including musicians (Amadeus Mozart, Franz Liszt), artists (Pablo Picasso, Akiane Kramarik), physicists (Wolfgang Pauli, Enrico Fermi), mathematicians (Ruth Lawrence), and writers (Alexander Pope, H. P. Lovecraft). It is a form of intuition that allows you to access answers without going through all the mental steps.

This ability can be a big issue for gifted kids in school as the teacher invariably wants an explanation of how they arrived at the answer. So they might be accused of cheating! Psychics use it to unlock meaning in abstract thought forms or to decode the structured packets of electromagnetic energy you have stored your information in. People with abstract intuition can have an affinity for music, numbers, formulae, sacred geometry, and spatial relationships—sometimes to the degree that they can listen to a musical score and re-create it or rearrange it without using the intellect; solve equations in their mind as symbols or numbers literally jump off the page and rearrange themselves; or conceive an architectural plan or new décor for their home as a vision without needing to draw it.

Imagine an apple. When you see an apple in your mind's eye, you are projecting the image energetically and observing it clairvoyantly. You might glean information from this symbol depending what it looks like. If it was held by a witch, it might be poisoned and represent danger. If it was bitten to the core, it might mean being out of options; or if it was very big, New York. So you see, the symbol of an apple can convey a lot of information. The idea of this apple could also be contained in a formula with precise information. That would let you unlock the apple's secrets and see how you might interact with it.

This is like what Nikola Tesla did in his mind laboratory.[21] He conducted experiments using his abstract intuition before doing them in physical real-

20. Wikipedia contributors. List of child prodigies. Wikipedia, The Free Encyclopedia, https://en.wikipedia.org/w/index.php?title=List_of_child_prodigies&oldid=893221665. Accessed April 30, 2019.

21. Wikipedia contributors. Nikola Tesla. Wikipedia, The Free Encyclopedia, https://en.wikipedia.org/w/index.php?title=Nikola_Tesla&oldid=894538767. Accessed April 30, 2019.

ity. It was the key to his success as a scientist. If you have this ability, you are more than likely aware of it already, unless you shut it down when you were young for fear of being teased and rejected because you were different.

Unlocking My Abstract Intuition

My abstract intuition is strongest when it comes to interpreting multidimensional symbols. My earliest memories of playing with this ability include seeing images in the clouds or the patterns of leaves in trees. Nowadays, I use it to read the energy of my clients.

I also express my abstract intuition through my art, which is colorful, whimsical, semi-abstract, and full of meaning. I am not a trained artist and so my paintings are childlike, but they are imbued with messages about spiritual awakening. My paintings pack much more meaning into a smaller space than I could express through writing. They are automatic drawings, in that I do not plan the composition with my intellect. I simply sit down and draw with no thoughts or preconceived ideas. When I do my art, I am operating at the interface between higher consciousness, which communicates multidimensionally, and physical reality.

These paintings started during a six-year period, when I was attending a modern-day mystery school, doing deep self-healing, intense energy practices, and emerging as an awakened human. I believe my paintings depict our journey of spiritual unfolding. They stimulate healing and spiritual growth and awareness within the viewer, because they bypass the intellect and speak to you as spirit. I have hundreds of these paintings. You can see some of them on my website gallery and on the Portico Soul Essence card deck.

Discovering Your Abstract Intuition

You could be experiencing some of the challenges associated with abstract intuition if you feel alone and it's difficult to meet others who can relate on "your level"; if you find everyday human interactions mundane, like they barely scratch the surface; if you see signs and synchronicities everywhere and link them together in ways other people wouldn't think of; or if you are intrigued by symbols because you can sense their meaning. Abstract intuition can be expressed in many ways; below are some more clues that this might be a psychic ability you have been using all along.

Sometimes a child with this ability is labeled as being gifted, or different. If your parents and teachers called you a child prodigy or wondered if you had autism, it's possible that your reality was being experienced through your abstract intuition. Even if you were not flagged as being different, but you won the competition to guess the number of beans in the jar, or were caught for cheating in class when you didn't do it, you may have been using this ability.

Perhaps you are someone with an uncanny knack for numbers, such as being able to easily remember strings of numbers, understand formulae, or solve complex equations with no effort. Or you love abstract representations of ideas, and surreal and symbolic art has deep meaning for you. Or reading, playing, and composing music comes easily to you. Maybe spatial relations and geometry are second nature, or you can see the underlying patterns in the natural world. All of these examples can be signs that your abstract intuition is at play.

Finally, if you enjoy playing with intuition cards, but don't need to memorize the instruction manual to interpret them, then you are using your abstract intuition to read the cards. Tarot decks can be a great way to train your intuition because they help you bypass the intellect. They are replete with symbolic information that can be unpackaged using your abstract intuition.

Gabriel Uses His Intuition at Work

Gabriel was having relationship difficulties. He couldn't connect emotionally with his partner and they could not agree about finances. They were locked into a pattern of passive-aggressive behavior. He was dissatisfied with his accounting career; he wanted to help people and felt there must be a better way than working for a corporate institution. He wanted to discover a higher purpose for his life.

Gabriel always knew he was different when it came to numbers. Ever since childhood, numbers would jump off the page and rearrange themselves into different patterns in front of his eyes. His highly developed abstract intuition is what made him succeed at his job, as he could instantly comprehend financial reports and investment portfolios in ways that confounded his colleagues.

As it turned out, Gabriel's purpose was related to everything bothering him. His relationship with his partner was teaching him about the emotional relationship people have with money. His job was teaching him about the financial system and its shortfalls. His abstract intuition gave him a perspective on finance that transcended logic and emotions.

This gave Gabriel a unique perspective that could be directed to assist people with their finances. Gabriel hatched a plan to teach money management. He would become an independent consultant, operating from sound financial principles and a desire to help shift the current financial paradigm and raise the vibration of our financial system.

Precognition

When most people think about psychics they imagine a fortune teller who can tell the future, which is either far-fetched or special, depending on their perspective. Yet this is an accessible skill that involves the sixth and seventh chakras. If you have ever had the experience of knowing what was going to happen before it did, you may have felt a sense of shock and awe. You also experienced a spiritual ability called *precognition* that allows you to intuit future events. The information you receive through this ability is known as a premonition. Premonitions can occur in waking reality or through your dreams. They involve information from the brow and crown chakras, helping you perceive future probabilities.

There is a long tradition of seers telling the future through dreams as well as other creative ways, from observing the flight patterns of birds to examining the entrails of animals. Famous seers include Edgar Cayce, Nostradamus, Mother Shipton, and the priestesses at the Delphic Oracle. In actuality, precognition is the most scientifically studied of all intuitive abilities. It is also the most practiced, with more than three hundred forms of augury (telling fortunes or the future through different types of creatures, practices, or object) recorded in the annals of history.

Studies have shown that many precognitive experiences occur in dreams and happen within a few days before a future event, although some occur months to years ahead of time. Most involve unhappy events, such as death, illness, accidents, and natural disasters. Intimacy is important as most precognitive experiences involve a spouse, family member, or friend. The rest involve disasters such as crashes or earthquakes and their victims.

If you are open to the idea that your larger consciousness is unlimited by time and space, then you may naturally be open to accessing future events from your waking consciousness. From our perspective in time and space, the future is a quantum field of possibilities. We navigate the moments of our life journey by making choices and using free will. So we can change what we see in a premonition.

Some psychics specialize in telling the future. They can be right when they tune in to the most likely probable outcome of a current situation. However, things can change, which is why they are sometimes wrong. They can also affect the outcome by causing their client to focus on specific scenarios, as you create your reality based on your beliefs, preferences, intentions and overall energy signature.

Precognition is actually an ability that is governed by the sixth and seventh chakras working together in unison. Future events can also be intuited in waking visions, auditory hallucinations, and sudden insights, and can be induced by trance, meditation, channeling, mediumship, and divination.

Visions of the Future

Years ago, I saw a plane crash in the Netherlands a few days before it happened.[22] I knew where it was because two friends who lived there were in the foreground watching the flames. I also saw a head-on collision between two fighter jets at an air show two days beforehand.[23] In both examples, I could not have guessed they would be real events; nor could I have foretold when they would take place. It was only in retrospect that I said, "Ah that is what that was."

I have also been introduced to new people who enter my life in dreams before I meet them, traveled to new places before I go there, and seen events

22. BBC. 1992: El Al jumbo crashes in Amsterdam. www.bbc.co.uk. http://news.bbc.co.uk/onthisday/hi/dates/stories/october/4/newsid_4617000/4617395.stm. Accessed April 2019.

23. Connet, David. 1993. RAF investigates jet collision at airshow: Organizers defend safety rules after fighters crash in mid-air. www.independant.co.uk. http://www.independent.co.uk/news/uk/raf-investigates-jet-collision-at-airshow-organisers-defend-safety-rules-after-fighters-crash-in-midair-1487196.html. Accessed April 2019.

from my own life played out in dreams before I experienced them in my waking life. There have been other dreams of crashes that never happened, other meetings that never transpired, and visits to astral realities that do not exist on the physical plane.

Many years ago, my parents were on holiday when my father's mother became ill. She was near death but hanging on. It had been impossible to get ahold of my dad to tell him. Yet when he walked in the door he said, "It's my mother, isn't it?" He explained that whenever a family member was close to death, he dreams he loses a tooth. I was amazed because I had the same dream. He said this was an old family dream from way back.

In general, I find it easier to recognize when there is a precognitive element in a personal dream than for mass events dreams. This is probably because I am closer to, and have greater control over, my personal reality and only observe or contribute as one of many in a mass event.

Your Precognitive Experiences

If you have ever had a déjà vu experience, where you felt you were experiencing something again that you had already experienced before, then you have had a glimpse into precognition. Déjà vu is a special case of precognition, which can be explained by the living out of an event that was first practiced in the out-of-body state. As the astral plane is unlimited by time and space, we sometimes try out different versions of things there before we manifest them physically. We will cover more about out-of-body experiences in Chapter 12.

The most common way people experience future time reality is through precognitive dreams. If you ever dreamed of a world event that later happened for real; dreamed about an illness (yours or someone else's) that was unknown at the time but later diagnosed; had a recurring dream that warned you of a future event; or met a person for the first time in a dream and then actually met them in real life, then you have experienced dream precognition.

You may have been tapping into this ability through your waking consciousness if you ever had a waking vision of the future; a premonition of an occurrence in your own life before it happened; the feeling you would bump into a friend and then did; had a premonition that someone was about to die or be in an accident and they were; believed you would be promoted or get a specific new job and then you did; or even knew in advance that someone would be visiting.

Other signs that you have precognition include scoring high in a PSI test where you had to predict what would come next, playing with tarot cards or similar intuitive tool and successfully predicting the future, having a body sensation that is a reliable predictor of something good or bad, doing something differently to avoid a possible future outcome, or even having the same premonition as someone else that was close to you. This is by no means an exhaustive list, but hopefully it is enough to give you some pointers in how to recognize this ability within yourself.

Elle Tunes in to Terror

One evening I was attending a party at a friend's house when I was introduced to an amazing woman. She had recently retired from being an investigator at an intelligence agency. This afforded her a lot of time to focus on herself and her inner world, and she told me her astounding story.

Elle had had premonitions for as long as she could remember. They usually came to her in her dreams. Now that she had more time, she was having them on a daily basis. She was keeping a dream journal and a record of what came true. She told me that, at first, she thought it was her imagination. Those she confided in were skeptical. But the investigator in her came out and she started sharing her impressions ahead of time with select family and friends. They were amazed to see stories in the news hours and days after Elle had reported the event. Here are a few of the many examples Elle told me about:

Elle saw a train derailment[24] on the TV news before bed on October 8, 1995. It was so vivid she told her ex-husband at 11 p.m. there might be work implications. The following day, the incident was reported in the news. The accident (considered sabotage) happened at 1:35 am on October 9. Elle witnessed it approximately two hours before it happened. Her ex-husband was the first verifiable witness to one of her premonitions.

---

24. Wikipedia contributors. Lac-Mégantic rail disaster. Wikipedia, The Free Encyclopedia, https://en.wikipedia.org/w/index.php?title=Lac-M%C3%A9gantic_rail_disaster&oldid=918627568. Accessed October 1, 2019.

Six weeks before the shooting on Parliament Hill in Canada on October 22, 2014,[25] Elle dreamed about the events in detail over several nights. She saw the gunman shootings and injuries and knew there would be an act of violence on Canadian soil because she saw a flagpole with the Canadian flag on a hill.

On March 7, eleven days before the terrorist attacks in Tunis on March 18, 2015,[26] Elle was sound asleep in her bed yet a part of her consciousness was transported to Bardo Museum in Tunis. She sat inside the bodies of various characters as the events unfolded. Later, when she watched footage on the internet, her experiences were played back to her; told by those same people whose bodies she had temporarily inhabited.

I asked Elle why she thought she was having these experiences. She told me that she was being opened up to different aspects of reality. It wasn't that she was supposed to (and couldn't) prevent disasters from happening. She didn't want to become a celebrity. It was more that she was supposed to teach people how interconnected we are through space and time. That we should value the lives we have now and approach experiences from spiritual values such as acceptance and forgiveness. We are all versions of each other, projections of the same source energy, playing out a vast drama to expand consciousness.

25. Wikipedia contributors. 2014 shootings at Parliament Hill, Ottawa. Wikipedia, The Free Encyclopedia, https://en.wikipedia.org/w/index.php?title=2014_shootings_at_Parliament_Hill,_Ottawa&oldid=893300217. Accessed April 30, 2019.

26. Wikipedia contributors. Bardo National Museum attack," Wikipedia, The Free Encyclopedia, https://en.wikipedia.org/w/index.php?title=Bardo_National_Museum_attack&oldid=890308684. Accessed April 30, 2019.

Chapter 10
INTUITION AND THE FIFTH CHAKRA

This chapter provides an explanation of the intuitive information flowing through the fifth chakra, also called the throat chakra, or Vishuddha. The fifth chakra, located in the cleft of the throat, allows a wide range of spiritual communication. I call it the spiritual chatterbox, as much communication takes place through this energy center. When you own it as spirit, you get to decide who to talk with as well as when and how you do it. You can discern your guides and other out-of-body beings and listen only to trusted voices.

When you don't own it as spirit, life will get confusing. Too many vibrations and voices will overwhelm you. You may be confused about which is your authentic inner voice versus the many external signals being picked up by your clairaudience and telepathic channels. You may lack confidence, fail to speak up for yourself, or even inadvertently express someone else's information. At the extreme side of this, you could believe you are crazy. This chapter will help you distinguish the various forms of fifth chakra communication.

While the fifth chakra is the communication chakra, all intuition is a form of communication. It is energy in motion and it always stimulates change. The change can include action but also new realizations and shifts in consciousness. Nothing can change if you don't communicate.

Psychic abilities covered in this chapter are inner voice, clairaudience, broadband and narrow band telepathy, and pragmatic intuition.

Inner Voice

If you talk to yourself, please don't be embarrassed. You are consciousness and your body is your vehicle for experiencing physicality. Your inner voice is you the eternal self, talking to your body personality. It is that still quiet voice inside that lets you hear your higher guidance. The inner voice sounds like you. It is a Trusted Source of information. It is the way you can receive answers from higher aspects of your own consciousness.

How clearly you can receive your inner voice depends on how strongly you identify with your illusory self and how much you open to the voices of others. Your ego is a construct of beliefs and behaviors that were created to protect you from pain. Unfortunately, your ego may be the dominant force governing your life. It is like a bandage covering the wounded child within. It might trick you into thinking it is your inner voice. You can tell the difference if you remember that your inner voice is always supportive. It will never criticize, judge, or say you are not good enough. It does not boast or compete or have you believe you are better than others.

External voices from other egos can make you unclear about your beliefs, desires, and information. Listening to them will feel confusing. If you listen to your inner voice, you will know what is right and true for you. You can ask your inner voice questions and listen for its answer. In time, you can learn which voices come from your brain, which come from other people who wish to influence you, and which come from your eternal essence. You can also learn the difference between your body's emotions, which are a communication from your body to your spirit, and your inner voice, which is a communication from spirit to your body-personality.

My Inner Voice Story

The way I tell the difference between my inner voice and the other voices flowing through my fifth chakra relates to the location of the communication. I don't know if it works like this for everyone, but I will share how it is for me in case it strikes a note. I experience my inner voice near my voice box. It sounds like me and it is aligned with the stream of consciousness that is me. I experience my clairaudience near my ears, and telepathy by my sinuses and sternum. I consciously adjust my fifth chakra to tune in or tune out, depending on which ability I want to use.

It wasn't always like this, and I experienced a lot of confusion earlier in my life. Other voices drowned out my inner voice and I had a lot of uncertainty about what I wanted to do. Many of the decisions I made were based on what other people wanted as opposed to what my inner voice was telling me. I gave my power away to the other voices. When my fifth chakra started opening up, I also experienced a lot of symptoms, especially a constant Morse code–like signal that was quite bothersome.

Eckhart Tolle's spiritual awakening, described in his book *The Power of Now*, is a testament to the power of the inner voice. The shocking realization that he had two voices conversing with each other caused a schism in his reality and thrust him into a rapid spiritual awakening. He spent the next few years reassembling. It doesn't have to happen in such an extreme way. For me, things got clearer and calmer gradually over a timeframe of years, without there being a crisis of consciousness.

Follow Your Inner Voice

There is a voice inside you that sounds just like you. This is your inner voice. It is a voice you can always trust. It is always supportive and gives appropriate guidance that will feel right to you. Once you recognize it, it can be hard to miss, but easy to ignore, unless you make a practice of paying attention to it. There can be so many other voices to filter out, including your ego, intellect, and other people's voices.

When we argue, the ego can have a tendency to be righteous. When your inner critic or outer judge is activated, they can override the inner voice. The intellect can be a handy tool if you're solving a problem, but if you limit yourself only to logic, and ignore the inner voice, you might not see all your options.

Let's look at some examples of how the inner voice might show up in your life. If you are physically attracted to someone, your inner voice might agree or disagree, but either way it is giving you a spiritual perspective on the situation. Your inner voice could guide you to make good financial decisions, or lead you to a windfall. It could help you make good career decisions, help you buy a new home, or offer guidance about a health condition.

If you are a spontaneous person who can act in the moment, you could be following your inner voice. If you can go against the pressure of expert opinions, or other people's recommendations when making big life decisions, you are also paying heed. If you still feel confident when a professional contradicts your inner voice, congratulations! However, if you need to seek a second opinion, or worse give your power away, then you do not trust your inner voice yet.

Blogger Discovers His Inner Voice

I read a blog article where the writer realized there were multiple voices in his head all speaking at once. He noticed different layers in his mind all conversing on different topics. After searching among them for a while, he identified a main voice that felt like him. He noticed he had control over it, whereas the other voices had a life of their own. Once in a while, his main voice wondered if the others could be quieted, but then he drifted off into thoughts about his relationship, his job, or the weather. Then a strange thing happened, the main voice shouted to the others to be quiet. They kept going regardless, making him feel frustrated.

He wanted peace inside his head but felt powerless to attain the meditative state he desired. Some days later, he was busy working, when all the voices suddenly stopped and for the first time ever he had a quiet mind. It was such an alien feeling it frightened him. Gradually, he learned how to cultivate this state of being. He discovered there was one main voice that he could hear and control once the din was quieted. This was his inner voice. Nowadays, he is able to focus his mind and ask questions directly to his inner voice. He receives verbal answers that are usually succinct and to the point. By listening, he knows he is on the right track.

Another acquaintance of mine believes all this spiritual stuff is poppycock. Yet even he has an inner voice. He is a very successful investor. Whenever he encounters a property that will make money, a trusted voice encourages him to purchase it. He has done very well by listening to his inner voice.

Clairaudience

If you think hearing disembodied voices means you are crazy, think again, it may just mean that you are clairaudient. Clairaudience simply means clear hearing and is an intuitive ability to perceive vibrations transmitted by beings without bodies, including spirit guides, angels, and other out-of-body entities, as well as people who do have a physical form. It allows for communication without the limits that time and space impose. So you can even use it to communicate with friends and family over long distances.

When my guides communicate with me, I hear voices speaking to me using language. Yet it is not like hearing physical voices. I also hear the music of the spheres from the angelic realm, but it isn't like earthly music. These are not physical sounds in the same way that you experience with your physical ears. They are more subtle, but they are real and can be distinguished from ordinary noises.

If you have ever experienced inexplicable sounds or people saying your name when no one was there, you may have been tuning in to your clairaudience. Clairaudience can frighten people, causing them to ignore or resist it, or fear madness. Hopefully, your experiences won't scare you, but if they do, don't despair. You can learn to screen out disturbing, unhelpful messages and listen only to Trusted Sources such as your angels and guides. After all, it would be a shame not to use this fantastic and fun communication ability.

My Clairaudience Awakening

My clairaudience has been a comfort during challenging times. Many years ago I hurt my back and had to stay in bed for three weeks. As I was recovering, I would take short walks and sometimes my back would give out and I wasn't sure I could make it home. Each time it happened, beautiful angelic music filled my consciousness and I felt reassured I would be fine. On another occasion, I was asleep in my hotel room on a business trip in Germany. I was woken by an angel singing at the end of my bed. While I don't know why it was there, it was a profoundly moving experience because of the beautiful music. There was no message, but I cried and as my tears flowed in some way I was healed from past hurts.

It has also been a curiosity. Once I heard the soap opera of an unknown gay man's life for months. I heard every thought and knew his every circumstance. Eventually, I realized what this background noise was and adjusted my clairaudience to stop receiving his frequency. Nowadays, I use it as a tool to talk to my spirit guides, especially my healing guides. I find it most helpful to listen to my healing guides' suggestions while my clairvoyance is focused on looking at and working on a client's energy.

Listening to Your Clairaudience

If you can hear sounds that other people cannot hear, close your eyes, think of someone, and hear their voice clearly, or play your favorite music in your head, using your imagination, then congratulations, you have been experiencing your clairaudience. If you suffer from ringing or tapping in the ears, it could be a sign that your clairaudience is starting to wake up. Although if concerned, you might want to see your doctor.

A common first experience of clairaudience is to hear someone say your name when you are drifting off to sleep, beautiful music when you are relaxing, or a voice warning you not to do something or reassuring you things will be alright. Other signs are if your memories include vivid sounds or if you sometimes talk in your head to friends and relatives about situations you have in common.

Even if you haven't had experiences you can put your finger on, if you use phrases such as, "I hear you," "sounds good," or "wake up and hear the music," that might suggest you are mainly auditory in both your psychic and physical senses. Other signs would be if sounds affect your mood; if, when you read a book, you hear the sounds of the scenes in your imagination; or, when planning for a future event, you hear what you and other people will say. Also, when you hear the words other people are thinking, that too can be your clairaudience.

Clairaudience and Musical Gifts

I believe there is a connection between the gift of clairaudience and musical genius so will share two stories that illustrate this. Luciano wrote to me about how he was hearing voices. He also heard original music in his head. This disturbed him as he was an academic and wanted a logical explanation. I told him he was receiving music from spirit. He learned about clairaudience and his fifth chakra. Now he has embraced a newfound gift as a musician and says he has a mystical muse, although he still wants it to make sense.

Debra Love was musical from a young age. She heard songs in her head that did not yet exist in the world. This made her feel different and she didn't know what to make of her experiences. At ten, she learned to play guitar. As an adult, she entered mainstream music and became an entertainer. She listened to the music in her head and began to write and record these songs. People who listened felt uplifted. The songs were pure and innocent and had the essence of the angels.

She was always very aware of the energy around her, including benevolent angelic guides and other less beneficial energies. She learned to use the power of her voice to clear the lower energies from her space. The angelic pop songs she wrote inspired Debra to explore healing and spirituality. She took a quantum-based healing course and became a certified healer. This propelled her into a period of intense growth. Lack of purpose was replaced by a realization that everything is energy. She realized she was a divine vessel, and setting frequencies and vibration was her gift.

The first song she channeled was called "Love." Since then, she has been given chakra attunements, devotional mantras, chants, and albums of songs that awaken and raise the frequency of the listener. She was guided to alter the frequency she tunes her instruments to. The standardized tuning is A equals 440 hertz. Debra uses A equals 432 hertz. This is a multidimensional frequency that helps elevate the human body to its highest expression of the divine self. Debra is constantly creating new divinely inspired music. She says it is a devotional process that includes healthy, clean, balanced living, which maintains her frequency at a level that allows such high vibrations to be birthed through her into the material realm.

Broadband and Narrow Band Telepathy

I wonder if the following experiences sound familiar to you. You have such a close relationship with your child, sibling, parent, or partner, you often know what they are thinking. You know when your friend, who lives on the other side of the world, is thinking about you. You're in a meeting at work and you can tell what your colleagues think of your ideas without them uttering a word.

Star Trek's Mr. Spock and other popular characters from film and TV are not the only ones capable of telepathy. It is a form of intuition we can all access with knowledge and practice. Telepathic experiences tend to occur with someone close. They are possible with pets and your preverbal toddler.

There are even scientific studies that support the existence of telepathy in humans, plants, and animals.

Telepathy is the ability to communicate through vibration without the spoken word and without body signals or sign language. You can send and receive spiritual information this way. The term is derived from the Greek words *tele* (distant) and *patheia* (feeling). You can use this ability to communicate spiritual information or perceive the vibrational signals of others. Telepathy is possible if the participants are close or far away.

There are two distinct forms of telepathic communication. *Broadband telepathy* is nonverbal communication with groups. Broadcasters or those speaking to crowds can be brilliant telepaths without realizing it. *Narrow band telepathy* involves communication with one or two individuals. Next time you become aware your dog wants a walk, you might be communicating this way.

Personal Experiences of Telepathy

Growing up I had a cat I loved very much. We were so close we could talk using mind pictures. One night I was lying in bed when I sensed she was in distress. I could see an image of one of her front legs being swollen, and felt she was unable to walk. I jumped out of bed and went to the back door to call her inside and see what was wrong. Once she arrived, at first glance she looked fine. When I looked closer, I realized her front leg was stuck through her collar and she couldn't walk properly. I untangled her, relieved she wasn't injured. I remember another time when she was ill and not eating. I sent the picture of her lapping up some milk and eventually she complied.

My first conscious experiences of telepathy occurred in childhood. My brother, father, and I used to play at sending thought waves to each other and guess what the other one was sending. It was a great game and we had a lot of fun with it. I played a similar game with friends to guess which colored pieces of paper one of them had hidden inside a box. As an adult, I have also used telepathy to ask plants where they wanted to be situated in my garden. When I follow my insight, the plants thrive.

Validating Your Telepathy

If you had the experience of being able to tell what someone else was thinking, having the same thoughts at the same time as those you are close to, having a habit of voicing what others are thinking, or tuning in to loved ones who are far away and instinctively know how they are, you have experienced telepathic communication. Some other traits that help identify a strong gift in this area include, being skilled at helping the tongue-tied express what they want to say, having a strong instinct about babies and their needs, or being able to easily understand and respond to your pets.

Telepaths often have a depth of understanding of others that most people don't share. They can pick up the consensus in a room of people who are debating a topic or read between the lines when someone is talking or lying. They are fabulous at nonverbal communication, and make great speakers because they can reach most people in a crowd by communicating beyond words. Their most common phrase is, "I was just thinking that" or "I knew you were going to say that." Telepathy involves receiving and sending. It can be easy for telepaths to influence and persuade others. Sometimes, they are vulnerable to foreign thoughts and have impulse to act out of character. If you identify with this description, you are telepathic.

Bruce is No Longer Scared to Speak

Bruce Starr is a fun, entertaining radio host. His Intuition Blueprint showed a strong focus on all aspects of communication, especially broadband telepathy. However, his telepathy was not operating at full potential at the time I did his blueprint. I discovered he was harboring the fear of death when it came to expressing how he felt.

Bruce lives in the United States but had lived in Central America for nearly ten years. In the country where he lived, the powers in charge were trying to control freedom of speech. He told me that he left the country after twenty television and radio journalists were murdered with none of the crimes solved. I believe he made the right decision as twenty-five more media journalists were murdered after he left. I worked with Bruce to help him learn how to let go of his fear of his past circumstances. We used the techniques in this book to reassure his body that he was no longer under threat and that it was now safe to fully express his beliefs. He has regained his confidence and has rebuilt his relationship coaching and speaking business as well as his public life as a presenter on radio and television.

Jimmy Found Purpose with Animals

Jimmy loathed his corporate job and needed a change. His Intuition Blueprint showed he was a capable communicator. During our Intuition Blueprint session, it emerged he had an affinity for animals. I saw he could help people understand their pets or livestock by being an animal trainer, intuitive, healer, or communicator. He even had prior lives where he mastered this ability, so he had the potential to be great at it in this life too. There was also a guide who had agreed to help him further develop his abilities. His goal for this life included using his skills in a more global way. Perhaps he could help raise awareness of how we impact plants and animals in the environment through our behavior and advocate for better balance.

The assistance Jimmy received previously did not help as the information was intellectual, not intuitive. He attended one-day workshops but lacked support to integrate or practice what he learned. Left alone, he invalidated his experiences. What helps people most is having someone to encourage them to keep going and validate that what they are tuning in to is real. Jimmy was delighted with his blueprint as it affirmed what he loved more than anything. He took a training program and is developing a coaching program to connect people with animals. He hopes to also help in pet bereavement services.

Pragmatic Intuition

If you've had the experience of knowing who was calling before answering your ringing phone, or if you could leave that parking spot three blocks away because you knew you could get one right outside the door, then you have experienced pragmatic intuition. A classic example of this form of intuition is bringing an umbrella on a sunny day or sunglasses on a rainy day, only to be vindicated by a change in weather later on. If you have had these surprisingly common experiences, it may not have been just a lucky guess. Pragmatic intuition is a form of intuition dealing with practical affairs. It helps you act on your information for practical gain.

Experiencing your pragmatic intuition is not necessarily about making a huge leap forward, having an amazing spiritual experience, or making an ingenious breakthrough. Instead, it feels more like plain old common sense. It helps with practical matters, such as short-term goals, next steps, and decision making. When there are a few variables at play in your immediate reality, pragmatic intuition can help you decide quickly and move forward with ease. If you use this type of intuition, you probably believe you are a practical person with good judgment. If you are not practical, it might just be that you have a fear of making decisions and are ignoring your pragmatic intuition, or that you have developed a pattern of doing what others say instead.

Saved by Pragmatic Intuition

One day I was scheduled to attend an outdoor celebration. On the morning of the event, the weather was bad and I decided not to go. This is unlike me, as I normally honor my commitments. Later that day, I heard that two trees had fallen onto the tents and the other participants had narrowly escaped injury. The wind made it impossible for the tents to stay in place so the event was canceled. My pragmatic intuition saved my day. If I had gone, my tent might have been under one of the falling trees.

On another occasion, I had an appointment at an office downtown. My boyfriend dropped me off and was supposed to wait in the waiting area. When I got out, though, he was nowhere to be found. After waiting a few minutes, I decided to walk. I instinctively turned right out of the building, then a right on the next street, and right again. There was a convenience store on my left as I turned, and I instinctively walked in. My boyfriend was there! This was an area of town we were both unfamiliar with. Neither of us had been at that office or store before. My pragmatic intuition led me there.

Your Pragmatic Intuition

Pragmatic intuition is a kind of everyday intuition that we often call by other names. If you are a very organized person, great at time management, always prepared for every eventuality, with an innate sense of how to get the best from people, you might be using this form of intuition to help you. You also might be using it if you tend to implement practical decisions versus procrastinating, immediately know what is possible given what is available to you, can easily separate what is possible from a pipe dream, and can readily condense group opinions into a practical course of action.

If you are a pragmatic intuitive, when life gets messy you can deal with it in a practical fashion. Your friends tend to come to you for advice on how to deal with stuff. Pointers that pragmatic intuition is at play in your life include having an uncanny ability to know who is calling when the phone or doorbell rings. Other signs this is in your nature include being able to figure out how to do practical things, such as change a tire, without instructions, or being the one who is relied on in an emergency situation. Pragmatic intuition can also help you get around more easily. For instance, being easily able to find your friends when you get separated, and changing your route while driving to avoid heavy traffic.

Other Pragmatic Intuition Examples

A mum I know uses her pragmatic intuition to be well prepared when she takes her baby out. I'm sure many other busy parents unconsciously use their pragmatic intuition to help them get through their schedule. I read about another mother who learned about pragmatic intuition from her toddler. Her son was attending a daycare center. He had just turned two years old so it was time for him to graduate to the toddler room, but he was hesitant and cried. She rationalized it, until she discovered that other parents were removing their kids from the toddler room. She realized he had intuited there was an issue, and she took practical steps to find a new location where he would feel safe.

Chapter 11
INTUITION AND THE FOURTH CHAKRA

This chapter covers the intuition of the fourth chakra, also known as the heart chakra, and Anahata. Located in the center of your chest, this communication center is a bridge between the upper, more spiritually focused chakras and the lower, more physically focused chakras. It interconnects you with everything, including source energy, humanity, and all creation. It can help you discern what is in vibrational alignment with your Trusted Source, life purpose, and highest good. Being in the center of the seven main chakras, it bridges higher and lower aspects of physical and nonphysical reality and balances dichotomies such as giving and receiving.

Experiencing your heart center can help you decide on a direction, set your course, and feel good about it. Your passion and desire can feel like a magnetic pull from your heart to a person, place, or thing. If something is in vibrational resonance, then your heart center will feel open and joyful. If it feels dissonant or you feel repulsed or repelled, then your intuition may be steering you in another direction; or your heart may be showing you where you are blocked, resistant, being protective, defensive, or limiting yourself.

Heart-centered feelings of attraction are known as affinity. Affinity helps you experience oneness, which is your connection with everything. In physical reality, you have the illusion of separation, yet you are connected with the whole of creation. The heart chakra can be open or closed to this interconnectedness, depending on what you believe or have experienced.

Heart-centered vibrations differ from emotions. They are forces of love, attraction, and cohesion. Emotions are feedback from the body about how it's experiencing reality, and can be experienced as pleasant or unpleasant. Both gut and heart can provide useful guidance to support your life direction and a balanced body-spirit partnership. Your heart has great power because it can connect you with all creation. It goes beyond this reality to all realities. It is a doorway to everything. It can connect you with every possibility imaginable for you, and your personal universe. Your affinity helps you connect with all that is. You can focus your heart's affinity to attract what you want. By resonating through love with what you consciously choose, you become a magnet for attracting it into your reality.

Intuitive abilities covered in this chapter are Affinity and Oneness.

Affinity

In human relationships, affection, passion, and enthusiasm are expressions of affinity. Passionate feelings about a person or a project are your affinity, providing information on encounters that are a vibrational match. Affinity lets you experience your desire to connect with others, attracts you to certain people, and magnetizes life experiences that resonate with your energy.

When in a state of attraction, you experience your affinity, whether you are enjoying socializing, engaging in a hobby, having a romantic date, communing with the divine, or lusting after a new sports car. Affinity works naturally if we allow it to flow. However, we can ignore it or block our awareness of it with expectations, judgment, nonacceptance, or fear of receiving the loving gifts the universe is offering.

Affinity is the cohesive force in our universe. You learned about it in school when your chemistry teacher taught you about chemical reactions and when your physics teacher taught you about electromagnetics. In astronomy, planets are kept in position by forces of attraction and repulsion. Just as the universe has a natural order, there is a fit for you in the cosmic consciousness.

Following My Affinity

Affinity is a force of nature. As a scientist, I learned about affinity when I learned about magnetic attraction, and the formation and propagation of life. Learning about it as part of my human nature is something that developed over time—mainly because when I was younger I was concerned with what others wanted of me, rather than what I desired for myself. There was a time in my life when I didn't know what I wanted because I didn't even realize I had my own needs. I was a people pleaser, my only function being to figure out what others wanted and not disappoint them.

I can look back over my life at many decisions I made that went against my affinity. I loved art when I was at school, but I chose a boring history class instead because I thought it would please my dad to show I was academic. I was depressed during my PhD, but I forced myself to plough on without seeking help. I chose a job in the United Kingdom with less money over a job I had been offered in Europe with more money and the promise of adventure, due to loneliness and the hope of fitting in, as opposed to loving myself and validating I could create my own happiness.

As I matured spiritually, I came to know and understand myself better. I made different choices about my life that were based on my intuition, and strength, rather than fear and weakness. I realized I deserved to have what I wanted, and I discovered what I desired. I finally got in touch with the affinity in my heart; and that affinity guided me in decision making that was in alignment with my highest and greatest good.

Experiencing Your Affinity

Someone who is experiencing their affinity will be guided by their heart in their relationships with friends and romantic partners. They will love spending time alone and with others, and be able to feel happy either way. When you follow your affinity, you might be strongly drawn to plants, animals, and the environment; naturally gravitate toward situations that are beneficial and supportive; or be drawn to people and situations that can help you. The universe seems to highlight things and events that are great for you. People who are not a match just fall out of your sphere of experience. You make choices in the moment based on what feels right in your heart.

If you can feel the divine presence of love vibrating within you, and can sense beauty in all things, including yourself, your life, and your body; if you are a passionate person who listens to your heart to make decisions, and knows whatever you want can be magnetized through your open loving heart, then I am preaching to the choir. You are already in touch with your heart's affinity. However, if you do not accept and appreciate yourself exactly as you are, you are not in touch with your self-affinity. Nor are you if you fear and judge others, do things to keep the peace or fit in, or don't know yourself very well and have no clue what you like—then there is work to be done in clearing this space.

Elaine's Self-Judgment Challenge

Elaine Cheung came to me for healing for her rheumatoid arthritis and a past-life reading to help with relationship challenges. She believed in commitment and fidelity, whereas her partner was exploring unlimited love and believed Elaine was misguided. The healing session showed Elaine's illness was fueled by high expectations, judgment, and lack of self-acceptance. Her background as a successful businesswoman made her take responsibility for everyone else in her life. The past-life reading revealed she had been an Essene at a time when her spiritual beliefs were unacceptable and meant she must hide. She began accepting that everyone has a different perspective and what is true for one may not be correct for another.

Through our sessions, she learned that by changing her beliefs and behavior she could change her life. I gave her tools to let go of foreign energy and see her relationship clearly. She realized her concept of love was unique and valid, but incompatible with her partners. Her affinity for a wider range of people and perspectives grew. She was thirsty to awaken her intuition. It was like watching a parched woman drink from a fire hose. As Elaine always wanted to learn new things, I stressed it was more important to use a few powerful techniques for inner healing and transformation than be perfect at doing as many of them as possible. She also wanted to know how well she was doing compared to others. I reminded her that everyone is different with their own purpose and talents; comparing her to other students did not make sense.

Elaine is now in a committed relationship and is dedicated to healing herself. She has her own healing practice and volunteers at a hospice. Helping people in transition can be a very emotional time, and Elaine's intuition helps her be neutral and compassionate without taking things personally.

Oneness

Oneness helps you realize you are part of everything and to sense where you fit within the whole. Oneness opens you to love and accept yourself and others. It relates to your connections with all life, including people, plants, animals, Earth, cosmos, divine source, as well as family, community, countries, nations, and nature. Everything that exists is connected. Oneness is your way to experience everything in the fabric of creation. Some refer to this as God, the great all that is, or source energy.

You are experiencing oneness when you feel integrated with all things and when you accept people and situations as they are without judgment or expectations. Experiencing oneness gives you the peace of mind that you are exactly where you are meant to be, doing what you need to do to fulfill your unique part in the symphony of souls.

If you feel lost like a black sheep, are constantly searching for your path in life, or question your place in the world, then you are out of touch with the vibration of oneness and out of alignment with source. When you are not in a state of oneness, you are not capable of unconditional love. Nor can you validate yourself, others, or the world in general. Instead, you might want what others have or feel responsible for them and try to give so much that you become sick.

My Experience of Oneness

It can be challenging to describe the feeling of oneness. It is a space where everything is. There are no emotions, apart from bliss and where all thoughts have ceased. As soon as you begin to describe it, you pull yourself out of the experience. From a personal perspective, I have been at one with all things through the practice of meditation. By allowing myself to simply be the consciousness that I am, and by expanding the radiance of my heart so that it engulfs my entire reality experience, I can sit in a state of peace and grace.

I also find that being in nature allows for this experience. I remember one beautiful sunny day basking on a rock by the ocean. The ripples on its surface were shimmering, there were boats gliding in and out of view. The sounds of birds and voices were on the wind. I was present and in an aware state. There was no thought, only pure presence of being. All these things I have just described were there and yet they were not there. There was no content or meaning assigned to any of it.

Earlier in my life, I went through many crises of self-identity. I didn't always know who I was, and was very concerned about what other people thought about me. I never felt good enough and worried about not fitting in and being rejected. I thought nobody loved me, and there was something wrong with me. All that changed when I learned to use the techniques taught in Part Three. I was able to clear away expectations, limiting beliefs, and foreign energy. The gift I unwrapped was me, and once I learned who she really was I loved her. Once I loved myself, I was able to love others and accept them as they are too. I was able to bring compassion and understanding to my teaching practice, as I have experienced within myself what is disturbing my clients.

Sensing the Oneness

To help you better identify with your sense of oneness, here are some signs that you are experiencing it: you have a high level of certainty about your feelings, needs, wants, and desires; even when physically alone, you don't feel lonely; and you know who you are, where you fit in, and why you are here.

Succumbing to other's expectations is a thing of the past. There is no pressure to fit in or match the energy of your family or other groups. You accept others without judgment. It is easy for you to appreciate them for who they are without needing them to change. You never try to emulate or compete with others, and when you sense others judging or criticizing you, you remain completely unaffected.

Your ego has been subjugated so your spirit shines through. Your spiritual practice includes accepting and being fully in the present moment. Whenever you look into the face of another, you see yourself staring back. You realize that everything and everyone is part of the same whole. Other people's interests and concerns are no more or less important to you than your own. It's easy for you to trust other people and situations you are in. You validate yourself and your place in the world.

Brice's Healing Crisis Opens His Heart

Brice Royer contacted me from his hospital bed. He was seriously ill and the doctors did not know what was wrong with him. He asked if I could send him some healing. I helped Brice on what he has since described as "the worst day of my life." As he couldn't afford to pay me, he offered his marketing expertise in exchange for healing, but he was so unwell that he needed to receive healing unconditionally. We both had to let go of a belief that you must receive back from the same person you give to or give to who you receive from (though he did help me later when he was well enough).

I didn't hear from Brice for a while. One day, I was reading the newspaper and there was an article about how he had turned his life around. It turns out he had a rare form of cancer. After researching environmental factors and their impact on health, he moved to a quieter location. He believed his problem was caused by an unsustainable economy causing stress, pollution, unhealthy lifestyles, and other factors leading to cancer. Brice felt he needed to separate himself from it before he got sicker. He believed the system was based on selfishness, greed, and accumulation. He founded a community based on unconditional giving and receiving. He learned that compassion improves your immune system and mental health; and he set out to help as many strangers as he could to heal his depression from his illness.

Pretty soon he was in the midst of another growth cycle. The more press he received, the more people came flooding in wanting him to take responsibility for them. This was a challenge and instead of relieving him it exhausted him more. He learned that not everyone is able to receive unconditionally and that unconditional giving and receiving are different from taking responsibility for others. While the journey has not been without hurdles, he helped many people receive things they otherwise could not afford. He opened his own heart and helped open other hearts through selfless acts of giving and the gratitude of receiving. Brice wrote the world's most-read Craigslist's ad "Unconditional Love For $0," which reached over a million views. He believes transactions using money isolate people but giving something creates trusting relationships and builds communities.

If you focus only on your heart chakra for guidance and interconnection, you can end up taking responsibility for others, merging with them energetically, and losing yourself. You can stay neutral and aware by balancing your heart with your upper chakras. Your seventh chakra helps you know yourself. Your sixth chakra allows you to be neutral and see what is in your best interests. Your throat center helps you express your personal truth. You can embrace the physical experience by balancing your heart chakra with your lower chakras. For example, your solar plexus provides the necessary energy for you to act on your desires.

Chapter 12
INTUITION AND THE THIRD CHAKRA

This chapter covers the intuition of the third chakra, also known as the solar plexus, or Manipura. This center connects you with your physical and astral bodies. It helps you distribute your energy where it's needed to support your desired life direction, whether you are pursuing a physical or nonphysical adventure or creation. As it is part of the Earth game to exercise free will, you must choose what to focus your energy on. Everyone has their own life force energy, to use as they wish in creating their life in this reality. Your third chakra distributes this energy in your physical and astral bodies. While you are infinite, you can only bring a finite amount of your energy into your physical body as the body is limited by time and space.

Intuitive abilities covered in this chapter are Energy Distribution, Out-of-Body Experience, and Out-of-Body Memory.

Energy Distribution

Your third chakra modulates the distribution of your life force energy so you can accomplish your purpose. What you use your energy for is always changing. During the day, you may need it to exercise in the morning, work in the afternoon, and socialize in the evening. Over a lifetime, you may need it to grow your infant body into an adult, have a child of your own, study at university, build a house, or negotiate a business deal. If you look back over your day, last year, or your entire life, you will see how your energy was focused in different ways at different times.

True power is really about you owning, balancing, and channeling your energy to consciously create your life. Unfortunately, many individuals misuse their energy to exert authority over others, believing they must compete to be successful or that there is always a hierarchy, whether at home, work, or play, so there is only room for one top dog.

You own your power when you live your life authentically. This requires enough self-knowledge to choose what you believe over what others say and to support yourself, regardless of others projections that would have you behave differently. You know what you want and ask for it. You know you deserve to be treated respectfully and have boundaries. When others behave badly, you are unaffected and can detach or walk away. By consciously remaining in your body and controlling your energy, you become more effective. You can turn your energy up or down; even direct it to your intuitive senses so you can determine where it needs to flow next.

My Energy Distribution Path

When I look back over my life, I am amazed at what I have accomplished. I have used my energy to gain a PhD, work as a scientist, and be a business developer. I used it to explore the world and adapt to living in different cultures. Then I switched focus to develop my intuition and heal myself. Now I use it to write spiritual books, teach intuition, and run a radio show.

In any given day, I am switching energy from one hour to the next. For example, today I am giving readings, healings, and mentoring students. I am teaching classes, writing and editing this book, preparing for an art show for my spiritual art, and preparing for my radio show tomorrow. I have discovered the key to being efficient and effective with my energy is to remain in the present moment, and to ensure I keep my energy field clear. That way, I can focus my energy through my body, like light flowing through a lens.

Your Energy Distribution

Let's take a look at how you use your energy and where you have it tied up. If you feel in alignment and use your energy to stay on track and fulfill your purpose, then you are using your energy wisely. You are focusing your life force energy units as was intended, to create your own reality, from free will in your unique way. There is no one else like you, and when you bring your unique vibration into the world, the heart of humanity rejoices because we get to experience the gift of you.

However, if you are a victim, intimidated by emotional assaults and dwelling on past hurts; afraid to stand up for your beliefs; don't trust yourself to make good decisions; uncertain about your wants; or feel manipulated, used, and ignored, then you do not own your power nor are you using your energy for your unique purpose. Instead, you are letting yourself be waylaid by invalidation, expectations, and limiting beliefs.

If you feel like a child being talked down to and told what to do; if you complain, but don't change anything; if you're a bully, imposing your will on others; or if you try to force change by competing with family, friends, or colleagues, then you are still tying up your energy inappropriately. It doesn't pay to keep everyone else happy at your own expense. If you are ignoring issues you care about because you don't think you can change them, or doing what others want to avoid rocking the boat, think again. This is not a recipe for empowerment or a purpose-filled life.

Nicky Reclaims Her Power

Nicky grew up in an abusive household. Her father was domineering, and the family was caught in the belief they must control or be controlled. She grew up with relatives who put spells on her and even attempted to possess her with their own energies so they could control what she did.

Given her background, it wasn't surprising that she doubted herself and gave her power to others. Nicky left home as soon as possible, but gravitated to abusive men like her father and created a series of failed relationships. She even joined a cult and could not tell her truth from theirs. Nicky was unable to make her own decisions. Only the priest could talk to God, and he held this power over her to make her obey.

I worked with Nicky extensively to help her clear the past experiences that kept her trapped in pain and powerlessness. She began to shift her victim mentality and take back her power. Her healing journey was not always easy, but over time, she got to know herself better. She can now discern her intuition from the desires of others, has reclaimed her power, and followed her knowing to create a new job and home.

Nicky is one of my most dedicated students. I have no doubt that she will continue to turn her life around and create the loving family and successful business her heart is set on.

Out-of-Body Experience (OOBE)

The third chakra governs out-of-body experience and out-of-body memory. You exist on multiple planes of reality and create bodies of different vibrations to experience them. While you may be most familiar with your physical body, it isn't your only one. You also have an astral body and light body, and exist as pure consciousness not in a body at all. You can have experiences in all your other bodies and in no body at all. The "you" associated with your physical body can become aware of other aspects of you in other realities.

The OOBE most people are familiar with is dreams, and this is what we will mostly focus on for the purposes of this book. There are two types of dreams. Those that are jumbled up thoughts or play back the day's activities are your body's way of processing its experiences. Dreams that have a timeline or definite storyline; dreams where time is fluid and you visit the past or future; or dreams where space is fluid and you go to other cities or countries are examples of astral travel and being on the astral plane.

The astral plane is an aspect of reality closely associated with Earth. It offers additional opportunities for you to expand your consciousness. When you sleep, your consciousness leaves your body and travels to other planes of existence. The astral plane is not bound by the same rules as physical reality. You can travel to the past, present, and future. You can be anywhere in an instant. A thought can immediately transport the astral body to any time, place, or psychological space you conceive. When you are in your astral body, you can fly, walk on water and move through physical matter.

The astral body is a vehicle you use in astral plane reality. It is less dense and of a higher vibration than the physical body. It offers more flexibility and greater creativity. It also provides more liberties when interacting with others and fewer limits. Astral travel is a form of out-of-body experience. Just as your physical body helps you focus on physical reality. Your astral body helps you focus on the astral plane.

Signs you are astral traveling include waking up in your dreams and consciously controlling your dreamscape; having lucid dreams; and having dreams of flying, being under the sea, or walking through walls. As you develop spiritually, you can learn to consciously astral travel, operate both your physical and astral body at the same time, and keep track of your astral body experiences through your sixth chakra.

My Dream Journal

My initial foray into the intuitive realm was through my dreams and I kept a dream diary for many years. In fact, I trained myself to record my dreams on a Dictaphone that I kept under my pillow. I slept with my finger on the record switch and as soon as I entered a REM cycle I automatically pressed record. The results were amazing. Some nights I recorded as many as five dreams. I only had a conscious memory of the last one, but there was my voice dictating my dream experience.

My nightly adventures intrigued me, as my dream reality behaved in opposition to the laws of physical reality I had been taught. I had premonitions of my personal life and world events, I met people I didn't yet know, and I experienced past-life scenarios where I recognized my friends even though they had different bodies. I allowed myself to be guided by my dreams and this is actually how I ended up living in Canada.

My fascination with dreams caused me to seek out those with a common interest. I trained in dream analysis, dream re-entry, and astral travel. My new friends introduced me to a school in the United Kingdom where I trained in healing and clairvoyance. In one lucid dream, I climbed a mountain and was instructed by a guide to jump without a parachute into the ocean. When I came for a job interview in British Columbia, I recognized Grouse Mountain and English Bay in Vancouver as the dream's location. I felt certain I was meant to go there.

I recall another experience, when I was on a business trip and very jet lagged. I had been reading *Seth Dreams and Projections of Consciousness*, channeled by Jane Roberts.[27] Seth had provided instruction, not only on how to become lucid in a dream, but also how to clear projections. The simple technique was to know you were in a dream and say, "Wake up now." As soon as I did this, the dream scenery completely disappeared and I was floating

27. Roberts. *Seth Dreams and Projections of Consciousness.*

close to the ceiling in a completely disembodied state. I could move around using my will alone. When I wished to return to my body I did, buzzing and vibrating as I entered it.

By the time I moved to Canada, I was already committed to my spiritual growth. Alone in my new country, I searched for like-minded people. I found an organization that offered advanced training in healing and intuition. As a result, my personal growth and spiritual evolvement accelerated. I now know how to use my astral body without entering the dream state.

Your Out-of-Body Experiences

If you are like most people, you dream and can remember your dreams. Even if you are one of the rare ones who claim they do not dream, here are some further clues that might help you identify your own out-of-body experiences. Flying dreams are a sign that you are astral traveling. Feeling like you are sinking, falling, or floating as you fall asleep are signs you are about to leave the body. Humming, buzzing, or clicking sounds as you wake up are signs of coming back into the physical body.

Some other common experiences include waking up and feeling conscious but being unable to move, or suddenly waking up with a jolt after an unusual dream. Other astral travel indicators include false awakenings, where you get up and go about your business, only to discover you were still asleep, and lucid dreams, where you wake up within a dream and are able to consciously observe what takes place, or even control what happens next. Sometimes, people are able to see a shining iridescent cord that attaches the physical body to the astral body when they are in this state.

If you ever dreamed you were wandering around your house just as it is in reality, except you were asleep, you have had a personal example of an out-of-body experience in the dream state. It is also possible to have out-of-body experiences while you are awake. Examples of this include feeling like your consciousness is not inside your body; waking visions that replace one reality with another; someone reporting seeing you somewhere, when you were actually somewhere else; feeling you're beside yourself or separated in two; or floating above your body when asleep or during an operation.

Shahiroz and the Crystal Skull

In 2012, my friend Shahiroz Walji ran a metaphysical store. At one time, Joshua Shapiro, author of *Journeys of the Crystal Skull Explorers*,[28] presented a workshop on crystal skulls. These artifacts were discovered in Mayan ruins and are said to be ancient energy transponders and storage devices. Joshua lent an original crystal skull to Shahiroz, who slept with it on her bedside table that night. She went to sleep and had one of the strangest experiences in her life.

She woke up, got up, and did her usual morning routine. Everything seemed real. Then she became aware it wasn't real and she was still asleep. This was evident when she suddenly noticed everything was glowing green. It looked like green laser lights flashing in all directions. She followed where they were coming from and it was from the crystal skull. At this moment, she realized she must still be asleep.

The next thing she knew, she rolled over in bed, yawned and got up. She had another shower, brushed her teeth, got dressed, and ate breakfast. Then realized she was still dreaming. She knew because the green glow was there again and she followed it back to the crystal skull once again. She lazed in bed a bit longer and then finally got up. Except she didn't! She was caught in her own crazy version of Groundhog Day. The cycle repeated many times, until eventually things were back to normal and the day continued as usual. Or as she says, did it? Perhaps she is still in the dream. Even normal crystals are powerful energy amplifiers. Because of her experience, for Shahiroz, the crystal skulls are off the charts!

Malcolm's Dream Comes True

Malcolm frequently has dreams with messages for his life. He also meets spirit guides and deceased loved ones in his nighttime adventures. He consulted me as he wanted assistance in understanding his experiences. I felt very qualified to help. As explained previously I trained in dream analysis and originally accessed my intuition through dreams before I learned how to do it consciously. Malcolm had such a high affinity for his dreams; his greatest wish was

---

28. Shapiro, Joshua. *Journeys of the Crystal Skull Explorers*. Kent: Washington Crystal Skull Explorers, 2018.

to be a dream interpreter. As he had great dream recall, we decided to work on developing his clairvoyance and knowingness so that he could more easily interpret both his dream symbols and those of others. His Intuition Blueprint had revealed a strong focus on intuitive seeing and knowing this lifetime, as well as trance mediumship (ability to come in and out of the body). He learned how to consciously see and know intuitively so he could know himself better, interpret his dreams to guide his life, and assist others to access their dream guidance.

Out-of-Body Memory

We do not recall all of our dreams or other out-of-body experiences. This is because they are taking place outside of time and space and in other realities. It would be impossible to fit these infinite experiences into a finite physical body. We use our out-of-body memory, located in the third chakra, to bring in relevant and useful information and to filter out experiences that are irrelevant to our waking consciousness.

Apart from dreams, the other form of out-of-body memory most people know about is a near death experience. There are lots of stories from people who experienced being outside of their physical body at a time of stress or trauma. Often they return with purpose and information to apply to their lives. Many of these accounts involve traveling down a tunnel to reach a bright light at the end. Scientists believe this is induced by changes in brain chemistry. I believe consciousness is moving through the dimensions of reality.

Memories from the Beyond

Stories of OOBE are quite commonplace, but in case you aren't familiar with any, here are some examples. A client of mine passed out at work. Her consciousness instantly shot into outer space. She experienced the wonder of the entire universe and knew she was an integral part of it. Another client left his body when he was in a car accident. He traveled into the light and was given the choice to return and complete a new cycle of growth in the same body.

My father hovered above the operating table as the disembodied neutral observer of his surgery. He could see and hear the medical staff as they went about their business. While recovering, he overheard the medical staff at the foot of his hospital bed say, "We nearly lost that one, didn't we?" They were shocked when he recounted what he had heard. A shaman friend uses out-of-body experiences for all his psychic readings and healings. He leaves the body, retrieves the information, and then brings back information to convey to his clients. Shamans have used this method since ancient times, in cultures all over the world.

Many people create a physical body and then ignore it or spend their life trying to find ways to get out of it. Sometimes a desire for astral travel can be a yearning to escape the pain of physical life. If you want to explore OOBEs, ask yourself why. I believe we are very lucky to live at a time of mass awakening, where we are being invited to access our gifts through the body in the waking state. There is no need to run away; you create your reality both inside and outside the body. If you have created something you do not like, you can heal it. In Part Three, you will learn meditation techniques that will help you do just that.

Your Out-of-Body Memory

If you don't remember your dreams, you may have an imbalance in the third chakra. Or your life is so busy and full that you do not currently have the bandwidth to bring your astral experiences into the body. If you would like to remember your dreams, then it can be a good idea to clean out the third chakra using the techniques presented in Part Three. Also, change your bedtime routine. If you can meditate and have quiet time before you go to bed, you will give your body time to calm down. Then before you fall asleep, set the intention that you will remember your dreams.

If you wake up feeling terrified or disturbed, it can be because you have brought a dream experience into the body that is irrelevant or inappropriate to this reality. The astral plane doesn't have ethics, like physical reality does. Nightmares can make sense from an inner psychological perspective, but they scare the body. If you are having experiences like this, learn to clean out the third chakra when you wake up, so that you do not carry the disturbance into your waking reality. Also, set the intention before you sleep that you will only bring back to the body that which needs to be integrated, and you will only recall what you need to know about to enhance your physical reality experience.

Tiana's Amazing Dream

While taking my Unlock Your Intuition psychic development course, a student had a wonderfully validating experience, which confirmed that her psychic abilities were unfolding. Tiana, who is a nurse, had a dream about a patient passing away. At the time of the person's passing, Tiana was at home asleep. In her dream, she was asleep, when another bed appeared at the bottom of hers. Suddenly, the person in the second bed sat bolt upright and tried to climb out of it. While unable to see the face, she immediately knew who the person was. She tried to assist them back to bed and notified the doctor. The setting then changed to a hospital room where a large cardiac monitor showed a heart rate and rhythm. Just as suddenly as the monitor appeared, the heart rate dropped and started to skip beats, then very quickly stopped altogether and went blank. Tiana called the doctor again who assessed the patient and pronounced her deceased. Coming out of the hospital room and back to the nurses' station, the clock behind the station indicated 1:05 p.m.

When Tiana arrived at work that night for her next shift, she found out the patient had passed away, and the doctor's notes stated she had been called to the patient for a dropping heart rate. It was a very quick turn of events and the situation was all over by 1:05 p.m., just as the dream portrayed. When Tiana recounted the story to me, she said she had felt that the person sitting up and climbing out of bed in the dream was the patient's spirit leaving the body. I believe a portion of Tiana's consciousness was in the room as the event transpired. Her story is a great example of out-of-body experience while in the dream state.

Chapter 13
INTUITION AND THE SECOND CHAKRA

This chapter covers the intuition of the second chakra, also known as the sacral chakra, or Svadhisthana. This energy center connects you with your physical body and creative energies used in self-expression and procreation. You sense your body's emotional, vibrational feedback throughout your life via this chakra.

The second chakra is the human relational chakra. It governs your ability to listen to your body's emotional and sexual signals, as well as those from other people. You are spirit. You have created a body. If you wish to follow your higher guidance, these two aspects need to communicate and work as an aligned partnership. The physical body has an intrinsic consciousness of its own (emotions, sex drive, intellect, physical senses). It is like a wild horse that spirit must tame, that is if spirit (higher guidance) is going to direct the life journey, which is done through the psychic senses.

The human form has an innate consciousness that responds on a vibrational level to its environment. It may respond with an emotion such as joy, delight, happiness, fear, anger, guilt, or shame, or have a sexual attraction to another body. In the nonphysical state, there is no sexuality or emotionality as we know it, there is no time and space and all exists simultaneously. Life on Earth gives you a chance to see the consequences of your creativity in a more focused way. The aspect of you that is incarnate experiences itself in time, space, and duality, where it takes time for the results of your actions to show up. Put another way, you get to experience the results of your action sequentially instead of simultaneously.

Most humans are trapped in the body consciousness levels, where the body's innate nature controls the experience. People get caught in emotional and sexual dramas, and intellectual loops. These things stop them from accessing their higher guidance. Clairsentience is the psychic ability that allows spirit to "read" the emotional states being expressed by the physical body. Spirit and body are meant to align in partnership and not fight against each other.

Most people use their clairsentience to check out how other people feel. This happens at a young age when you ask yourself, "Is Mummy sad?" "Is Daddy mad?" "Am I safe?" However, its primary purpose is to help you develop a relationship with your own body. If you don't use it for that, you may feel overwhelmed because you are busy dealing with other people's emotional energy.

Remember, you are an eternal being of pure consciousness. You have projected an aspect of your consciousness into a physical body to experience Earth reality. If your body likes your current choices, it will tell you by responding with a higher vibration emotion. If not, it will let you know through an unpleasant feeling. Your role is as an awakened presence offering guidance. When you listen and respond to your body, it will trust you. Then your body personality will align with you and your life purpose.

There is a single intuitive ability covered in this chapter: Clairsentience.

Clairsentience

Clairsentience helps you comprehend your body's emotions. You use it to relate and respond to your body's reality. Clairsentience is often referred to as being an empath. A simple way to think about it is your emotions are sending you feedback about yourself, your situation, and other people. Clairsentience is the intuitive sense that allows you to pick up on that. If you have ever had a gut feeling, then you've experienced clairsentience. In fact, most people use clairsentience every day without realizing it, especially as it also lets you sense how other bodies are feeling. You may already be using it to tune in to family, peers, and colleagues. Next time you sense how a friend feels without them telling you, pause and notice this type of intuition.

Your body emits a range of emotional frequencies to respond to your experiences. In essence, there are two main states, positive or negative, meaning all emotions feel good or bad. You can embody high vibrational states by healing your body. You can also catch your body spiraling down the emotional scale and work with it to feel better. Emotions are your feedback loop. They are a guidance system that helps you make course corrections. They are communications from your finite body to you, the eternal being.

Imagine your body is a sensing device you placed on the end of a line and dropped into the ocean. It tells you if the water is warm or cool, if the current is strong or weak, even what kind of fish are present. If it sends a high vibration signal, all is well. If not, the opposite is true. By sensing into your body, you can find out if you need to modify your life circumstances to accommodate its preferences. Perhaps it is grumpy as you have been working too hard and it wants to sleep or exercise. Or it's anxious because of a difficult relationship. The body is a pleasure-seeking device. It naturally wants to go to higher vibrational states that feel good. It prefers not to feel pain and needs you to move it to a better feeling emotion by being responsible for it. If you do not, it will figure out a way to cope, but that could involve drugs, alcohol, sex, television, or other distractions.

As the body operates in time and space, it may take time to process its experiences, so it is helpful if you can be patient. Even if you can't make an immediate adjustment to disturbing circumstances, you can acknowledge what your body is saying and tell it how you plan to change. If it is frustrated at being stuck in traffic, you can play soothing music rather than create a downward emotional spiral by allowing negative thoughts. If you are grieving a loss, then give your body time and space to adjust, rather than denying your feelings so you can get on.

If you ignore your body's signals of unhappiness, it will take matters into its own hands. It won't trust you. It may even kick you out of the body causing you to you feel unfocused. Then if it can't sort things out through ego, emotional tantrums, or the intellect, it will shout louder by developing a physical disease instead of an emotional dis-ease. If you are exposed to people who invade your space, your body will respond by being afraid, angry, or sad. By listening to its signals, you can decide to own your space and remove yourself from the unpleasant situation. If you are in an unpleasant job or unhealthy relationship but not ready to leave, then explain your reasons to your body and find ways to help it cope with it when things get bad.

The body responds emotionally to thoughts. Dissonant thoughts impose on the body's view of reality. Your worries and negative thoughts seem real to the body, even if they only exist in your mind. Thoughts can even cause feelings of pleasure at the expense of another person. This is why the mind, body, spirit relationship is important—so that spirit can heal the damaged ego.

While the main purpose of clairsentience is for you to communicate with your body, many people use it to be hyper-vigilant around others in order to stay safe. Being sensitive to the emotions of others is a common issue. Empathic people feel overwhelmed because they do not own their personal space. Their confusion is because their emotions are mixed with the emotions of others. Clairsentience can help you discern which body the feelings you are experiencing are coming from. You can use it to become familiar with different energy signatures so you know if this is Mum, Dad, or me.

As we have seen, there are many challenges to consciously using this ability as it deals with the strongest pulls of the physical body. Most people live their lives being pulled into emotional dramas or sexual attractions. Meditation is important for owning your space and accessing intuition. To master clairsentience means that you the spirit must take charge of your body; you must learn how to deal with the body's animal nature and let go of other people's energy.

My Clairsentience Experiences

These days I am very neutral because I focus my consciousness in my sixth chakra, and have been doing so for over twenty years. Before I knew how to do that though, my life was a bit of an emotional roller-coaster ride. This was usually due to not having a relationship, breaking up from a relationship, or feeling misunderstood in one. As a child in my nuclear family of four, there were often angry outbursts and people storming off. I recognize now that as a family we were so merged energetically that we each could feel the others disturbed energies. In the work I do now, I see this is very common and occurs in most families.

It is a major challenge for most people on a spiritual path to clear their parents' energy from their space. In fact, it took me years to gain seniority over this. I remember when my teacher told me that I needed to make separations from my family I was outraged and thought she was instructing me to hate my family. I didn't understand the concept of owning my space at all. Owning your space is not a rejection of those you love. It is a gift to release their energy and give it back to them so they can use it to create their own life. It is a blessing to be able to own your energy field and use your own energy free and clear to create the life you truly want.

Given the work I do, it's very important for me to do my daily energy hygiene and clear the foreign energy from my space. Otherwise, I can end up feeling emotions that belong to my clients. Though I have seniority over this because of my use of my sixth chakra, it can still be uncomfortable to channel an emotion that doesn't make sense in my reality. When this happens, it is usually because there is something inside me that matches the client's experience, so I use it as a way to direct my personal healing process that day.

Your Clairsentience Experiences

Business people validate clairsentience when they follow their gut instincts about a business deal. Counselors do it when they get a split-second instinct that helps a suicidal patient. Parents do it when they sense something amiss with their child. If you rely on your gut feelings, this is a sign that you too are using your clairsentience. If you have this ability, it might be easy for you to put yourself in other people's shoes. You are likely sensitive to the emotions of others without them saying how they feel—so your friends rely on you to be empathic when they are experiencing emotionally heightened situations.

The flip side is you can end up feeling other's pain in sympathy for them. You can be an emotional sponge, and feel overwhelmed by conflicting emotions, some of them yours and some of them from others. You can feel excited or fearful and not know why. Or you can experience aches, pains, and other unpleasantness with no apparent cause. Crowds can leave you feeling overwhelmed and drained.

When your space is invaded with other people's emotional energy, it can be hard to express your own emotions, make decisions, and put yourself first, and sometimes it can put your body into fear and cause you to lack emotional control. This ability has many challenges, but seniority with it is most helpful in building a strong, healthy partnership with your physical body. It can be very helpful to learn how to make energetic separations from others. Then you can feel confident and clear, and be more discerning about your own energy versus that of others.

Marika's Emotional Challenges

Other people left Marika feeling drained. Emotionally expressive people confused and overwhelmed her. She had issues setting boundaries with friends, family, and boyfriends. This resulted in many emotional outbursts and arguments. Marika was empathic and wanted to explore how it could enhance her life. I taught her some meditation techniques, and we worked extensively on her second chakra to help her let go of the past and foreign energy.

She had picked up programming from her parents to please others and put their needs first. By clearing out limits caused by the pain of feeling unworthy and unimportant, we were able to unblock and activate her clairsentience. She used it to communicate with her body so she could heal her relationship with it. She began to understand the difference between love and sex, merging and togetherness, as well as how to own her energetic space from others.

Her challenge became a gift when she mastered her second chakra. She now uses her clairsentience to help women with their reproductive and sexual health. Marika became a doula to help women during pregnancy, birth, and postpartum. She is sensitive to the needs of mother and baby and has developed expertise in shamanism and healing to soothe health issues that come up. She also studied Chinese medicine.

Trang's Stress Relief

Trang had a high-stress job in a mental health facility treating clients living with severe mental illness. The high demands of the job left her feeling physically restless, drained, and overwhelmed. She also experienced severe monthly migraine headaches causing her to miss work, which affected her productivity. Mentally, she found it increasingly difficult to organize her thoughts and communicate her ideas, which became an ongoing source of sadness and frustration for her.

After taking my Unlock Your Intuition psychic development course and practicing the techniques taught in this book, Trang became aware of the negative energies that had accumulated in her energetic field over the years. The subsequent release of these negative energies helped her to gain clarity and feel more at peace. Her anxiety slowly melted away and in its place, she felt confident and empowered.

Trang is now able to relax, pursue her passions, and enjoy life. She no longer suffers from monthly migraine headaches, and the migraine attacks have been reduced to approximately one to two times a year. She is also able to utilize the skills learned in the class to remain calm and neutral even when confronted with challenging situations at work. Her intuitive skills became heightened, allowing her to trust her own inner guidance. By taking my intuition development class, she discovered how to access information that aids in her self-awareness and drastically improves the quality of her life.

Sharon's Anxiety Marker Disappeared

Sharon took my intuition development class while receiving neurophysiological treatments from her anxiety doctor. She had experienced anxiety her whole life. It stemmed from many things, including being attacked by a dog as a child. After one or two classes, she told me she had an appointment with her anxiety doctor. After he finished the testing, he looked at the numbers then told her she had erased one of her markers for trauma. He said her brain had become very plastic and was responding quickly. The only thing she did differently in her life to explain the change was to meditate using the techniques presented in this book. She said it was interesting to see a positive indicator in black and white and have a doctor comment on it.

Sharon became so passionate about energy healing that she has been training to be a healer herself. She has used bioenergy healing to relieve even more of her anxiety symptoms and to help her husband heal from irritable bowel syndrome. Sharon says her road to healing has been one of many incremental steps, and she knows she is headed in the right direction, as she continues on her healing path. Anxiety has had such an impact on Sharon's life, she hopes that sharing her experiences of different approaches and their results will help other anxiety sufferers.

Chapter 14

INTUITION AND THE FIRST CHAKRA

This chapter explains intuition governed by your first chakra, also called the root or base chakra and Muladhara. The first chakra is your connection to physical reality. It governs survival of the physical body and your relationship with planet Earth. This energy center helps you interact with the low vibrational frequencies of solid matter. This includes being aware of your environment, and assuring survival and maintenance of a healthy body. This survival instinct is a type of intuition. We will also discuss the feet chakras because they relate to your connection with Earth energies.

A purpose of planet Earth is to sustain life in physical form. We can learn many things by observing how she balances nature. She supports our expansion and provides a playground for us to transform ourselves. We raise the vibration on Earth when we ground via the first chakra. By anchoring light in the material plane, we light up the world. A planet of awakened humans is a planetary body with a very high vibration. Ungrounded humans can't do this, as they are not consciously present in their bodies. The energy we anchor to Earth by grounding "fertilizes" life and maintains the health of our world and flow of life.

Our bodies are crystalline. Being mainly water and minerals, we can absorb, generate, and transmit electrical charges. Essentially, we are transmitters and receivers of energy. Just think how rubbing your hands together can generate static electricity, or the school science experiment where you hold hands to complete an electrical circuit and switch on a light. You step down higher vibration energies through your chakra system all the way to the first chakra, which connects you with physical reality.

All of us together form an interconnected matrix of transmitters and receivers who channel the energies that form our mass reality. The aspect of you that deals with Earth plane reality is referred to as the lower self or body personality. You are unique and have unique information accessible through all your chakras. As you explore your first chakra, you may encounter fears and blocks. You can work with your body to clear them until you can operate it without disruption and bring yourself fully here to create your life consciously as spirit. We are the opposite of astronauts, who journey from Earth to the stars. We come from the stars to Earth, take on a physical mantle, and learn to navigate unfamiliar terrain while wearing our Earth suits.

The intuitive abilities covered in this chapter are Body Survival Instinct and Earth Reality Instinct.

Body Survival Instinct

Your first chakra channels survival information, including a template for healthy cells and organs. When injury, pain, and discomfort trigger survival signals, information on how to respond is available through your first chakra. There is a kind of innate intuition within your cells in that they respond to your thoughts and beliefs. You can actually believe yourself healthy or sick. Your DNA will respond to your intentions to be fit, energized, and well. A great way to heal your body is to own your space so that your energy and information is flowing freely through it. Anchoring the light of your consciousness to physical reality is necessary for you to be an awakened human.

The survival instinct refers to your ability to ensure your survival needs are met. That means your basic life needs such as air, food, drink, shelter, warmth, and sleep. Depending on the location in space and time for your incarnation, different information might be channeled. Living in the desert is different that living in the Arctic. A concrete jungle is a different environment compared to the actual jungle. It follows that a hunter gatherer has a higher focus on physical survival than a wealthy royal, as would someone born with a chronic health condition versus someone who is born healthy and strong.

Your first chakra is associated with the gonads and contains information concerned with the survival of the species. Your second chakra also relates to reproduction, but more from the perspective of sexual expression. Your conception, gestation, and birth can impact how you use your first chakra through your lifetime. A loving conception and easy birth may result in the belief that the physical world is safe and fun. Sexual abuse and a complicated labor may cause you to believe the physical world is very frightening. It can be important for you to heal this trauma so that you can access your survival instinct free from limiting beliefs.

When you are first born, you aren't capable of surviving without your mother. You rely on mother's instincts until you can fend for yourself. The relationship with your parents can color your interaction with the world in a positive or negative way, as can the political, religious, and cultural environment that surrounds you. They all program their followers with survival-based beliefs such as codes of dress, vows of poverty, tithing income, fear of eternal damnation, no contraception, no medical intervention, male and female roles, and what days to go to work. Governments levy taxes to provide for safety in the form of emergency services, health care, old-age pensions, benefits for single mothers, and welfare for the unemployed. Cultural groups tell the history of wars and the common enemy. Relatives tell you about things that run in the family.

You have your own innate survival information, but if you do not own it, you can end up creating your life through pain, punishment, and other limitations. You also have a unique concept of the divine. Any authority that intervenes with that relationship interferes with the expression of your first chakra, and your unique information on how to live your life in physical reality. Meditation is a great way to get clear on your information and to let go of concepts that come from outside of you. As the age-old tenet says, "The Truth Shall Set You Free." For only then will you be free to choose your unique path.

My Survival Stories

I have had many near escapes from disaster. When I was a scientist, I worked at a research station in Ecuador. There was a civil uprising while I was there; all the roads were blockaded, people were kidnapped, cars were torched, bombs exploded in hotels. The army refused to help us. We could not leave and missed our flight home. The high altitude made me dizzy and made my nose bleed. Altogether, it was a miserable situation. By the time the uprising was over, we were surviving on rice and ketchup.

On another occasion, I contracted enterocolitis, followed by a bad reaction to the drugs the Ecuadorian doctor prescribed. The ordeal lasted over a week and culminated in an emergency situation on the flight home. Luckily, a Dutch surgeon onboard treated me, though not before he made me sign a waiver that he wasn't responsible if he killed me by injecting the incorrect dose of a drug from the plane's medical kit. I came to peace that I might die in that moment. At least that seemed better than continuing to suffer.

I've also had a string of near disasters while scuba diving. There was the time my dry suit valve stuck open on a deep wreck dive, launching me to the surface like a cannon ball. Or the time when sunshine turned to a storm while we were in the water, making it almost impossible to get back to land. Or the time when the dive boat couldn't see us drifting out to sea on a strong current, leaving us no choice but to climb onto some rocks and be rescued. Or my very first open-water dive, where I was left alone at the bottom of a 25-meter gravel pit, never having done an ascent and without the proper equipment to do it. Luckily, I was eventually rescued.

In reviewing all these stories, I've realized they all come from the time in my life before I knew how to meditate and before I healed myself by clearing foreign energy, expectations, and limiting beliefs. I have altered my vibration significantly since then, and I haven't attracted a survival emergency in years. I no longer do things based on peer pressure or demands from authority figures, all of which played a significant role in the list of stories above.

Your Story

Review your life so far and reflect on your unique survival instinct. You might have stories like mine. Or you may discover information about your relationship with money, health, home, and career, as these all relate to survival. Whenever you identify a limit, ask where it came from. You might have picked it up from your parents, siblings, teachers, or peers. Then reflect on whether it is in agreement with your personal truth.

As mentioned, the people who had the biggest influence over your belief system were your parents or the people who brought you up. As an adult, you may still be operating from your mother's or father's beliefs about how to survive. If these were limiting beliefs, then they will limit your ability to meet your basic needs and create what you want for yourself as an adult.

Here are some examples of limiting beliefs you might resonate with: Life is a struggle. You have to work hard to earn money to survive. You must compete against others to get more. Women earn less than men and do more work. Women must look pretty and use their sexuality to survive. Your intellect, emotions, or sexuality is what matters most to survive. We must all look and act the same and create our lives in the same way. You are responsible for the survival of your group. Survival of the family is more important than that of the individual. Women and children first, men must sacrifice themselves.

Some or all of the above might apply for you, and you might come up with some other ones. Make a note of them all and use the techniques you will learn in Part Three to help you release them.

Alanna's Survival Challenge

Alanna was being harassed at work. She was depressed as she wished her colleagues would accept her. She thought that if she knew what motivated them she could change them. Although it was difficult to hear at first, Alanna eventually realized the only person she could change was herself. She used the techniques in this book to release self-judgment and cultivate acceptance of herself and others.

As she changed her internal environment, her external environment shifted. Soon she had created a new job where her colleagues were friendlier. However, her troubles were not over and she soon faced another challenge. She became embroiled in a situation where she was broke and could lose her home. She had no one to help and went on welfare. Luckily, she remembered to use the techniques.

Alanna focused on clearing everything within that had attracted her misfortune. Her situation changed once again. As she shifted inside, she attracted more stability. As she described, "I had to surrender to the universe and quickly manifest a better situation. Now I know what it's like to surrender and truly trust in my manifestation. I 'saw' the perfect person I could live with and unexpectedly ran into her. Actually, it was like I knew I would in a way."

Earth Reality Instinct

Your feet chakras allow communication between you and the planet. They draw vital forces from the planetary body and circulate them within your physical and energy bodies. Your physical body is a cell in the larger body of Earth. Just as your cells are inter-dependent with your body systems, your physical body relies on the planet for health and well-being.

Connecting to Earth through your feet chakras embeds you in Earth's reality matrix and allows an energetic exchange with Earth's energy grids. You can discharge energy into and receive energy from Earth through your feet chakras. When these chakras are not functioning well, you won't feel connected in the here and now. When open to Earth energy, you are plugged into planetary conditions. You can ride the waves of change and adjust to global and local energy shifts.

This is especially important in this time of rapid change in our world. You are alive at a time when the planet's energy has been shifting exponentially. You chose to be here now, as this time-space reality offers an unprecedented opportunity for evolvement. Knowing about Earth energy helps you make the most of it. By running Earth's energy through your feet chakras, you attune your creativity to the creative impulses on the planet. You ensure your life is in balance and that whatever you manifest is in alignment with Earth.

Wherever you go on Earth, you integrate local energy within your system and add your unique energy signature. Earth uses your gift to create, maintain, and evolve the natural environment. Nature shares local Earth energy so you can make adjustments and be in balance with what surrounds you.

The feet chakras are closely associated with your first chakra. You can ground to Earth through your feet chakras and first chakra. This creates a very stable foundation for physical existence and can be comforting for the body. When grounded, you anchor light. Part of your purpose as an awakening human is to anchor your unique frequency of light on Earth. When plugged into Earth and source, you help raise the frequency of the planet, shine a light on the world, and connect with other bright sparks through the planetary grid.

My Earth Walk

Many world traditions talk about Earth's energy grids. The Australian aborigines go on a walkabout along ancient songlines, while European pilgrims travel ley lines to visit sacred sites. Chinese walk on dragon lines; Americans walk on spirit lines. I like to think about all the places I have visited on my Earth walk. I have lived and worked in six countries and traveled to a much larger number for work and leisure.

I am sitting in my native England as I write this with its soft undulating landscape and layers of history. My village has been inhabited for 8,500 years and is one of the oldest in the United Kingdom. It certainly feels very different from the wide open spaces of Canada where I currently reside. My favorite energy site is Copán in Honduras; it is a place where I felt cradled in the hand of God. My least favorite site is a high-altitude desert in Ecuador, where I felt I might die if I remained there too long.

Your Earth Walk

My feet have touched Earth in many places, assimilating her transformative energies and magnetic currents. My feet chakras have amplified and regulated the quality and intensity of Earth energy into my personal energy field with every step. Yours have done the same. Take a moment to consider all the places you have been on our planet. Remember what the energy was like in these different locales, and recall which were your most and least favorite energy spots and why.

Guardians of Earth

I met a man after giving a talk on intuition. He had won a psychic reading session with me. It was one of the most interesting readings I have ever given. It turned out he was part of a group who worked with the energy grids of Earth to keep it balanced and healthy. The group he worked with were aware of research that was harming the natural cycles and weather patterns, and they were doing energy work to counterbalance the damage.

Sarah, a client of mine, was living in the far north near a mountain range where ancient legend said there was a special location that contained information for the benefit of humanity. The local indigenous population knew of its existence and that they were its wisdom keepers. Unfortunately, some of the knowledge had been lost during the time when foreigners invaded their land.

Sarah became aware of past lives when she and her son had been ancestors of these people. She was able to recall the knowledge from her Akashic Record through meditation and past-life sessions with me and is now working with the local First Nations community to unlock the secrets of this ancient repository of knowledge. She has become dedicated to creating the necessary space for open communication and for validating its importance.

Chapter 15
MULTI-CHAKRA
INTUITION

In order to comprehensively explain intuition, I have broken the information down into bite-sized pieces, based on each chakra. However, each chakra is not an island. It is part of a system that functions together.

The capacity of the first chakra extends beyond survival. The capacity of the crown chakra extends beyond knowing, and the capacity of the sixth chakra beyond seeing.

In Chapter 9, when we discussed precognition, we explored what happens when the sixth and seventh chakras are coordinated. Yet this is not the only form of multi-chakra intuition. A spiritual master can go further than the limits of our perceived physical laws to perform miracle healings, levitate, walk on water, manipulate matter, manifest instantly, and even disappear or blend into nature like the Cheshire Cat.

This chapter is devoted to the psychic abilities that draw from the power of more than one energy center. These chakras help you navigate and manipulate energy in physical form, and cooperate to sense and influence energy for balance, healing, and change. We will also introduce the hand chakras and their role in manifestation, because they are also involved in the forms of multi-chakra intuition.

The types of intuition and their associated chakras discussed in this chapter are Healing, Telekinesis, Psychometry, and Manifestation.

Healing

You comprise electromagnetic energy organized in specific patterns, including your auric field, chakras, and energy channels, also called meridians or nadis. Energy flows through them to support your organs and other body systems and help maintain health. Blocks in the energy flow can be caused by you holding your energy in unhelpful ways as a result of mental, emotional, or physical trauma, or because you are in resistance and have nonsupportive beliefs about your reality.

Healing is the process for creating change in your physical, mental, and emotional state, beliefs and energy flow so that harmony is restored and resistance is cleared. It draws on information from your hand chakras and your sixth, seventh, and first chakras. Fundamentally, all healing is self-healing. You must want to shift to be healed. A healer catalyzes change by providing you with energy or a new way of looking at the world that reconnects you with your source, but it is ultimately up to you to receive and use the energy and information.

By opening your intuition, you can access a world of unseen energy. You can claim your power and create change using intention. Whether you want to change your body or life circumstances, there are many healing modalities to explore. If you are passionate about change, then you are a healer—whether you want to clean the environment, improve the healthcare system, be an energy healer or make people laugh.

Personal Healing Anecdotes

I have been a professional energy healer for over twenty years. I've been doing it so long and worked on so many people that it's hard to single out examples. Yet I would like to briefly share my most recent experience and discuss my evolution as a healer. I don't follow a specific modality because I use my intuitive abilities such as my clairvoyance and claircognizance to inform how I work with each individual. I see what is blocked and use energy and intention to help clear it. I frequently perform aura, meridian, and chakra healings, astral body cleanouts, head channel healings, female healings, entity removal, medical intuition scans, ancestral clearings, energy retrievals, clairvoyant and long-distance healings, and anything else that is required to assist someone. Just like using my clairvoyance for psychic readings, doing energy healings is second nature to me.

I also consult with my healing guides. Many healing guides have come and gone over the years, so many that I have lost count. I have worked with ascended masters, archangels, devas, galactic beings, and many other spirit friends. Depending on what my focus is in my personal growth and energy practice, I align with helpers who can best assist me. I even sometimes recruit guides to help my clients. I am very rarely taken by surprise. However, one evening in the spring of 2018, I was enjoying a warm salt bath when I was taken out of body by two star beings. They trained me to activate silent DNA that has been dormant in humans, until such time we become sufficiently evolved in consciousness to access it. Since then, they bring me people to work on who are ready for this next step in human evolution. Suffice it to say my journey as a healer has never been dull. You can learn more about my readings and healing at my website, as referenced in the About the Author section.

Discovering if You Are a Healer

Here are some signs you are a natural born healer: The idea of being a healer excites you and you are attracted to alternative healing modalities. You imagined being a doctor or a nurse when you were a kid. You think a lot about how you can help others, and care more about making a meaningful contribution than anything else. You immediately rush to comfort people in distress, or visualize healing energies when you pass the scene of an accident. When someone close has a minor hurt, you place your hands on the area and rub it better. You can sense energy with your hands or you feel energy flowing out through your palms. What is more, you seem to have a knack at knowing what ails someone, and can intuitively sense when someone close is unwell.

Some other tendencies can include feeling responsible to raise the spirits of everyone involved, when a situation feels uncomfortable; feeling angry at injustice and unfairness; or being a magnet for people seeking support and having a tendency to take on everyone else's problems, and putting their needs above your own. Healers can be really good at looking after plants and pets as well.

Cress Heals Herself First

Cress Spicer told me that the biggest challenge on her journey to become an energy healer was being overwhelmed by the amount of work she must do on herself. Early in her career, Cress noticed she was accumulating her clients' issues and this was triggering her. She realized the practice of working as a healer creates much personal growth and she must heal herself first. As each client brings the opportunity to look in the mirror, she must stay on top of her personal healing to able to help them.

Cress also told me she was once plagued with self-doubt and still has to perform inner healing on being judged and not accepted for expressing her creativity as a healer. She constantly works on expanding her consciousness as she believes this makes her a better healer. She says, "I truly believe to work with others we have to be clear in ourselves."

Another learning she shared relates to setting boundaries. She needs time and space for herself, her family and personal healing. This should be balanced against the needs of clients. Cress has been learning to let go of responsibility for others or else she loses her space and everything falls apart. She has also learned that her clients must want to heal and believe that they can. If they expect her to take on their problem, then the healing process doesn't work.

Cress is most grateful for her deep connection to spirit and her grounding to Earth. Connecting to the planet has helped her manage her energy and increase her sensitivity. The more she has healed herself, the more authentic she becomes and this is reflected in her healing practice. She says it is always a work in progress that there is no ultimate level of attainment. Rather, we learn how to manage our energy so we can deal with challenges more readily. Cress loves what she does. She has found her life purpose and would not have it any other way.

Angela Works on Her Faith

Angela is a healer. She has learned many modes of healing and has a passion for herbalism. She has a constant battle with her daughter, however, who is a scientist and will not listen to anything she says. Her daughter reckons she is insane for believing in healing. Angela and her daughter had chosen their relationship to learn to tolerate others beliefs and to validate their own without needing to judge, convert or disempower others.

An additional challenge for Angela was that she struggled to make enough money as a healer. So she went back to college to study to be a dental hygienist. When Angela had her Intuition Blueprint done, I validated her purpose as a healer and her passion for healing went beyond this lifetime. Her main struggle was in having faith in herself. We worked on changing her belief that it was not possible to create abundance doing what she loved, or that she had failed by taking a mainstream job. We also worked on her ability to manifest, which was another area where she was blocked.

Telekinesis

Telekinesis is the ability to move objects using mind power. Telekinesis means "distant-movement." It refers to the ability to move or change the state of an object by using your thoughts without using physical force. It can include causing an object to move, shake, vibrate, spin, levitate, or even break. It draws on information in the hand chakras and your sixth, seventh, and first chakras. Using telekinesis, you can create heat or cold in an object via the speeding up or slowing down of the atoms it is made of. You can also manipulate energetic frequencies such as light, radio waves, magnetic waves, and electricity.

At present, telekinesis is not a common ability on Earth. However, legends speak of ancient ones who could blend with the energy in trees, rocks, and water and even manipulate forces of nature such as wind and fire. Consciously controlling matter involves mastery of several energy centers as you need to be able to visualize or mentally conceive the desired result and channel the energy frequencies necessary to cause the change. Synchronization of conscious intent with the energy waveform of an object can cause it to be reconfigured.

There are similarities between healing and telekinesis as they both involve transforming energy frequencies. The difference is that telekinesis tangibly affects solid matter in real time. An example of a healer using telekinesis would be someone who is able to dissolve kidney stones. Whereas a healer not using that ability might help shift the mental and emotional levels that caused the condition in the first place.

Not everyone is telekinetic. If you have this ability, you will be able to move things with your mind. So if spoons bend in people's drawers when you visit or if clocks and watches stop in your presence, then you might be telekinetic. A fun way to test this is to put a pencil at one end of a table and yourself at the other end. Concentrate on the pencil, and move it toward you using only willpower. If you make it move at all with only your mind, then you likely do have telekinesis and may be able to learn to do more.

In ancient times, telekinesis was used to move massive objects to create buildings and erect monoliths. You may be incredulous but just think about all the indigenous cultures performing rain dances. They were wise and knew they were connected to nature and that energy follows thought.

My Telekinesis Tales

I've never been able to lift a stone with my mind, but I can dissolve clouds and there have been magical moments when I swear I have been able to increase or still the wind, invite the rain to stop, or stretch time. When I was studying to become a spiritual teacher, I would drive from Vancouver to Seattle every other weekend for my classes. I always arrived on time, no matter when I left home. If I overslept or something else happened to delay me, even when it was impossible to do the journey in the time available, I focused on bending reality to get me there on time.

Richard Bach, who wrote *Jonathan Livingston Seagull*[29] and *Illusions, the Adventures of a Reluctant Messiah*,[30] is one of my favorite authors. I learned about cloudbusting from him. I used to enjoy lying on my back at the beach on a glorious summer's day looking at the images in the clouds. Then I would choose the smallest, puffiest one to dissolve and gradually move to larger and larger clouds. My old house had a lovely deck overlooking the back garden, where we would sit on long summer evenings. I remember one occasion when the dusk was rolling in and the weather started to shift. There was wind and a light sprinkling of rain. I used my mind power to calm the wind then rustle it up again. I did this repeatedly. It was a fun game.

29. Bach, Richard. *Jonathan Livingston Seagull*. New York: Scribner, 2014.
30. Bach, Richard. *Illusions, the Adventures of a Reluctant Messiah*. New York: Dell, 1989.

I've definitely had clients with bigger telekinetic powers than I have. My own father couldn't put a watch on his wrist without it stopping, or running too fast or slow. We had some great family fun attempting to bend spoons, or spin compasses while watching Uri Geller[31] on television. It's not something I ever managed to do.

Could You Be Telekinetic?

If you are attracted to the idea of moving objects through willpower, or if objects, such as your keys, inexplicably move from one place to another, then you might have this ability. Other examples of telekinesis in action include watches running fast or slow when you wear them; clocks, televisions, electrical equipment, and mechanical devices stopping when you are around; or being prone to computer crashes.

When you are angry, if you have noticed accidents occur around you, such as drinks spilling and glasses smashing, even though no one touched them, this could be due to unfettered telekinetic ability. It can be put to positive use as well. For instance, start up a broken item by wishing or willing it to be fixed.

If people receive electric shocks when they touch you, if it is easier for you to move heavy or awkward objects than it is for others, if you can make a compass move by willing it to, or if you find bent cutlery all the time, then you could be exhibiting signs of this rare ability. At least give the cloudbusting a shot. At the very least you will have some child-like fun and that can't be bad now, can it?

Sylvio Stops the Bus

Sylvio arrived late for his appointment with me. He appeared both frustrated and concerned. He said he was having trouble traveling around and wanted me to look at what was going on. He didn't have a car, so he traveled on public transport. Lately, every bus he got on inexplicably broke down. It had happened too many times to be a coincidence and was interfering with his ability to get around. He believed it must have something to do with him. On this particular day, the first bus broke down. Then the replacement bus

31. Geller, Uri, and Lyon Playfair, Guy. *The Geller Effect*. New York: Henry Holt & Co, 1987.

stopped working. Even when the buses didn't break down, the electrical lights blinked.

I saw intuitively there was a connection between the breakdowns and his telekinetic energy. Energy pulses were arcing off his energy field and impacting electrical appliances around him. He was shorting out the circuits. I told Sylvio to gain control of his energy by increasing his grounding; so the excess energy was directed away safely. I also looked at his thoughts at the time that the incidences happened. He was feeling stressed and uncertain about his life. It seemed the incidences coincided with his most stressful moments. Once he started associating himself with the transportation breakdowns, this only added to his stress.

Sylvio learned to use the meditation techniques presented in Part Three to help relieve stress. He adapted his abilities so that they could be used in a way that gives him joy and makes more sense. He now focuses his intuitive abilities by working in herbalism.

Psychometry

Psychometry means soul measurement and is the ability to intuitively read stored information in objects. It is also called clairtangency, and is the main ability used in pendulum work and dowsing. Psychometry lets you know the history of an object by touching it. Information pertinent to this skill is channeled by a combination of energy centers located in the brow, crown, and palms. They work together for you to feel, see, and know about the history of an object. Psychics sometimes use this ability to do readings for people, either by holding a photograph, more usually a favorite piece of jewelry, or a frequently worn article of clothing. The reason being, when you wear an object it absorbs your energy, and then transmits it as part of its energy field.

Objects exposed to emotional or physical intensity from their owners and frequent users hold an energy charge, allowing you to pick up images, histories, and impressions by holding or touching them. If you tried but your experiences were vague, don't be discouraged. Keep practicing. Using a pendulum can be a great way to begin to explore psychometry. You can start with yes or no or two choice answers to your questions.

If you are particularly sensitive to the energy fields in nature or connect with the past through objects and buildings, then you may already be experiencing this ability. In which case you might like to try the ancient art of dowsing, where twigs or rods are used to locate groundwater, buried metals, ores, gemstones, oil, and graves without the aid of scientific instruments. It can be used to follow ancient ley lines in Earth's energy grid and feel power spots or energy vortices in the landscape.

My Built-In Tour Guide

I love visiting ancient sites. When on vacation, I never hire a tour guide. Instead, I use my psychometry skills to tune in. When allowed, I touch a wall or a statue and read the history stored in the object. Often, my information supports the official information. Other times it is different. It is always fun! One of my favorite places on Earth is the British Museum in London. My favorite part is the ancient Egyptian relics. I discovered I can read the history of the statues. Some contain "spells" for growing crops or the health of the people. They also have a series of Mayan panels, which are fascinating to me. They depict ritualistic scenes that relate to kundalini, which they called the vision serpent, as well as artifacts from all over the world from ancient to more recent history. Museums are a great place to try out your own psychometry skills.

Your Psychometry Skills

Anyone can learn to use this ability, but if you are particularly sensitive to the energy fields in nature or connect with the past through objects and buildings, then you may already be experiencing psychometry. Everyone is unique, so while your experiences may be vague and undefined, your way of perceiving is no better or worse than anyone else's. Don't invalidate your experiences based on the expectation that they should be vibrant, detailed scenarios. Here are some tips to help you identify the kinds of experiences that are due to this ability.

If like me, you have ever been to a historical site and felt like the walls were telling a story, if you enjoy antiques and love to imagine their history, or if you've been in an old room or house and felt uncomfortable, then your attraction or repulsion might be telling you something. Perhaps you are a really tactile person who likes to hold objects in your hands to get a sense of them. For example, you have sensed the prior owner by feeling a used object, a piece of inherited jewelry makes you feel closer to a deceased loved one. Perhaps when you look at old photographs of people, you can intuit something about them.

Maybe when you're shopping and need to decide on a purchase quickly, you make your decision by touching the objects, or you already own a pendulum and this is one of your favorite tools for making decisions about food and nutrition. If you do energy clearings on your house and surroundings, own a dowsing rod and have been successful at sensing water or other energies, feel attuned to nature and the land, and have a fascination with ancient monuments and ley lines, then these are also big clues of your psychometry ability.

My Friend the History Buff

A long-lost friend of mine used to work in an auction house. His job was to evaluate and value the incoming objects from estate sales and other sources. Most objects he handled were very old and had been owned through generations of the same family or had many owners over the years. He had the gift of psychometry and would frequently go into a reverie about the object he was holding. He was able to see its history, including the people who had owned it and the rooms that it had occupied. He found it fascinating and because he had such a keen interest in antiques would wander around the image of the rooms where the objects had been housed with his psychic vision to see what else was there. He had to be careful to do his job in a timely fashion, though. He could spend far too long with objects that were particularly fascinating to him.

Reading the Past Through Objects

I read about a renowned psychic of the twentieth century, Stefan Ossowiecki,[32] who had a strong gift for psychometry. It was said he had an eighty percent success rate when performing psychometry on sealed envelopes to determine the writing or drawing inside. He displayed amazing abilities with archaeological objects and described the lives of prehistoric humans by holding a ten-thousand-year-old flint tool. After the Nazis invaded Poland, hundreds of people came to him with photographs of missing family and friends.

---

32. Ian Stevenson, Zofia Weaver, and Mary Rose Barrington. *A World in a Grain of Sand: The Clairvoyance of Stefan Ossowiecki*. North Carolina: McFarland & Company, 2005.

He tried to help them discover what had happened. He also predicted his own death before the end of the war.

Manifestation

Manifestation refers to your ability to create your own reality. You do this unconsciously until you learn to do it consciously. Your creative energy flowing through your hand chakras is used to create in this reality. This makes sense when you think about it. You use your physical hands to create all the time, whether you are cooking dinner, driving your car, or writing a note.

There are energy channels in your arms, where creative and healing energies flow. This energy emanates from energy centers in the palms of your hands. It flows out into the world through these centers. They help you create the energy blueprint of what you are manifesting. They channel your healing energy, and help you sense energy. By feeling the energy, you can determine how you might like to change it. Your hand chakras help you to give and receive. Usually your dominant hand is the sending hand and the other is the receiving hand. This is most evident in people who are energy healers.

Everything in your life is your creation. What manifests for you relates to your energy, intentions, beliefs, thoughts, and actions. It is great to be aware of this so you can change them if they don't support what you want. There is also a close relationship between speaking and manifesting. In the Book of Genesis, God speaks the world into being. Spells and incantations are uttered in order to manifest some form of result. Saying your intentions aloud, visualizing them, and imagining yourself to already have them help you to consciously manifest.

My Manifestation Tales

The last module of my Unlock Your Intuition psychic development course focuses on teaching conscious manifestation techniques and on clearing blocks to manifestation. I ask my students to create a manifestation list and use these techniques to create what they want. They share a copy of the list with me, and I hold onto it for three months. When the time is up, I send the list back to them to remind them what they wanted. By this time most people have forgotten. When they receive the list, they are often shocked to see that much of what they had asked for has already shown up in their life, or at least there are positive signs they are on their way.

If I look back on my life, I can see I was a very determined little girl. I used my strong will and ability to visualize so I could pass exams. When I took my final exams for my Bachelor's degree, I broke out in hives all over my hands. This was clearly a block in my creative energy flow. I did pass, but all that information crammed in and bursting to get out, coupled with the stress, made for a painful and itchy time.

One of the key turning points in my life was the first time I was laid off in a corporate downsizing. I was devastated and I swore I would create a life where no one could ever again have that level of power over my reality. I had recently been to a psychic fair and was amazed at my experiences there. I knew that was what I wanted to do. I remember sitting and crying and willing that I had my own business doing readings. This manifestation did not come about for another twelve years, after intense self-healing.

Things I desire manifest much faster these days because I have done a lot of work to clear my energy field of blocks and resistances. Take this book for example. There are so many stories of amazing authors such as J. K. Rowling who have their manuscript rejected by hundreds of publishers before their work is published. An author I interviewed on my radio show told me his agent found him a publisher on his first try. He made me believe this was possible. I decided I wanted to create a publishing deal as easily as he did. Llewellyn was the second publisher I sent this manuscript to. They enjoyed it and decided to publish it.

The time it takes to manifest something is proportional to how much you doubt it can happen. If you can clear doubt, fear, resistance, and other blocks and replace them with desire, joy, belief, and expectation, you will be amazed at how quickly things can happen.

Find Out if You Are a Good Manifestor

The ingredients to conscious manifestation include the following steps in the creation process. First, knowing what you want. If you deny your needs, give your energy away to others, and have no clue about what to manifest, you won't score high on the conscious manifestation scale. If you do not believe you can have what you want, you will fall down due to feelings of self-doubt, low self-esteem, and unworthiness. Second, your creativity is supported by spirit. All you have to do is speak up and ask, but for some people asking for what they want and trusting the universe to provide for their needs isn't easy. Third is letting go and allowing the universe to do its work. This means not trying to control your creations, and not setting limits on exactly how they must be delivered.

If you are not limited by any of the above challenges, then you are doing well. Stand by and be prepared for what happens next. Recognize your creation when it comes. Having expectations on what your creation should look like places limits on what you allow yourself to receive. If the universe delivers a blue-eyed lover, but you want a brown-eyed beauty, you might turn away a fabulous partner. Allow yourself to have. Some people are great at creating what they want but have issues deserving them so they will not let themselves receive their creations when they arrive. Enjoy your creation. Some people only experience their creation for a moment before it slips through their fingers, or they don't allow themselves the luxury of enjoying what they created. Instead, they bypass it and move on to the next thing.

Andrew Lets Go of Manifestation Blocks

When meditating on how I could best help Andrew, I intuitively heard him say, "I put the world in my heart and now my heart is missing." His main challenges were taking responsibility for others, judgment, and giving so much that he was unbalanced. Andrew was a natural-born healer who also had blocks in manifesting.

It is a common issue for natural healers to take on the energy of those they wish to heal. This is due to the mistaken belief that they have more power and healing ability than their subject so they must take on other people's wounds to heal them. This doesn't help the healer or the person being healed. It just means that the healer's space accumulates other people's pain and they start creating their reality through it.

Andrew's energy was going more to helping others rather than for himself. Plus, when he did create something, he didn't hold on to it for long. He ended up giving it away or allowing others to take it. He had a judgment about being taken advantage of over money, especially as he was going through an acrimonious divorce. His business was impacted by his pain and he wasn't attracting as many clients as before.

As we talked through his issues, he shifted his perspective. He realized that by taking responsibility for others he denied their growth and invalidated their ability to heal themselves. It made him unbalanced in his giving and receiving. Andrew still struggles to let go of his judgment. Especially when he sees others creating through their pain and hatred. If he gets stuck, he comes to me and we work through it together. He has developed a spiritual perspective on his life and is grateful to have a mentor to help him with his growth.

Part Three

FIVE MEDITATION TECHNIQUES FOR INTUITION DEVELOPMENT

Chapter 16

MEDITATIONS TO
BE PRESENT

You cannot master your life purposes, chakras, and intuition unless you are truly present in your physical body. Being in your body brings you into the now moment, where you have the power to fully participate in this reality as an awakened human and conscious co-creator with source. This chapter provides instruction on how to consciously walk on Earth as an awakened human, present within your body.

Your physical body is always in present time. It cannot be anywhere else. It exists in three-dimensional space. You may believe you are present in your physical body, but this may not be correct. Many humans are actually quite disconnected from their bodies. In fact, this is common in spiritual circles because of the desire to connect with vibrations of spirit, which are much higher than the body vibration. It is also common for people to not be fully in this reality because they are escaping their pain.

My favorite metaphor for demonstrating this is traveling in a vehicle from A to B. As you left your house you were conscious you had to go somewhere. You were aware of getting ready and leaving. You may remember opening the car door, getting in, sitting down and even turning the ignition. However, on arrival at point B, you have no recollection of how you got there! Surprisingly, a great many people have this experience, especially on a route that they take every day. It's so familiar they sleep through it. If this has happened to you, you did not remember the journey because you were not present in your body while it was happening.

Even if you sit at home all day without going anywhere, I am sure you have had the experience of spacing out at your computer or television. All your awareness is sucked into the screen and hours can pass by. Or you have day dreamed during a boring meeting, then scrambled to reconnect with reality when someone spoke to you. In moments such as these, you are not awake inside your body, so how can you be aware of your purpose, master your chakra system, or receive intuitive guidance?

Breathing Techniques

There are many different schools of meditation. One thing they all have in common is the breath. When you tune in to the breath, you are focusing on your body and therefore are in the world, right here, right now as that is where your body resides. You can simply breathe in and out rhythmically and deeply, feeling the belly and diaphragm expand on the in breath and contract on the out breath. Or you can practice one of many breathing techniques that were developed in the different meditation traditions. Two techniques shared below are square breathing and ascending breath, but there are many others for you to explore if you wish.

SQUARE BREATHING

Square breathing, also called box breathing, is a very simple technique that helps you reset your energy and clear distractions. It is very easy to do:

- Breathe in for 4 seconds
- Hold for 4 seconds
- Breathe out for 4 seconds
- Hold for 4 seconds
- Repeat 4 times

ASCENDING BREATH

Ascending breath is a yoga practice that is very good for calming the mind, connecting you with your body, and helping you relax. To practice this technique, sit or lie down so your head, neck, and spine are straight.

- Exhale from the top of the head to the toes, and inhale from the toes to the top of the head.

- Next, sequentially exhale and inhale from the top of the head to the ankles, then knees, perineum, navel, heart center, throat, and finally the bridge between the nostrils.

- Breathe in and out several times at the center of your forehead.

- Follow the above sequence in reverse: bridge between the nostrils, throat, heart center, navel, perineum, knees, and ankles.

- Finish by breathing as if exhaling from the top of the head down to the toes, and as if inhaling from the toes up to the top of the head.

A calm and steady breath is an important underpinning to the ancient mystery meditation practices that I teach. The first and foremost technique I teach my students is grounding from the first chakra. It should be accompanied by deep breaths in and out; as should all the techniques taught in this book.

Grounding Techniques

You the spiritual being have a very high vibration. Your body, which is made of dense matter, has a much lower vibration. To access your intuition and be in an enlightened state of consciousness, you must connect these two states of being. A great analogy is to think about electricity. All electrical devices are grounded as a way to safely channel unused current. Otherwise, the electricity would leak into the appliance resulting in electric shock. Have fun for a moment and imagine your friends and family as electrical appliances. Some are blenders whirring around and turning everything to mush. Others are like toasters, warming things up nicely, or freezers, bringing a chill wherever they go.

Everything is energy including you. Different people have different vibrations. Yet you all have one thing in common: your consciousness is like the electrical current and your body the appliance. All electrical appliances have a grounding wire. It makes it safe for electricity to flow through it. If there is an unexpected electrical surge, the excess current is grounded off. To safely stay in your body and not arc off into the stratosphere, you must install your own grounding cord. Grounding is a powerful transformational tool that anchors you, the high-vibration consciousness, into your physical body so that you can take charge of your life.

The grounding technique helps you be more aware of your body and its experiences in the physical world. It focuses your attention in the here and now. You become more present and aware when you are grounded. This makes you stronger, more stable, and in charge. It makes it safe for you to be in your body. Being grounded, present, and aware helps you know yourself and why you are here. It is the first step in mastering your chakra system, consciously activating your intuitive abilities, and using them as an awakened human. The best way I know to ground is by creating a conscious connection between your energy and the center of Earth. Below is the grounding technique I teach, which I first learned from my spiritual mentor, Mary Ellen Flora.[33]

GROUNDING CORD MEDITATION

- Sit comfortably with your feet on the ground, a straight back, and your hands in your lap.

- Take a deep breath in and out, and continue a slow steady breath throughout your meditation.

- Be aware of your first chakra, which is an energy center near the base of your spine.

- Create an energy connection from there to the center of the planet.

- Imagine an energy cord that is securely fastened at the base of your spine and at the core of the Earth.

- You are now grounded.

- Relax and experience your grounding.

    - How is your body responding to this exercise?

    - How do you feel about being grounded?

    - Allow your own unique experience.

33. Flora, Mary Ellen. *Meditation: Key to Spiritual Awakening*. Everett: CDM Publications, 2000.

- Release your grounding to see how you feel without it.
  - How is your body responding now?
  - How do you feel about not being grounded?
  - Allow your own unique experience.
- Once again, create a grounding cord from your first chakra to the center of the planet.
- This time, think of a word that describes how you feel.
- Be aware if this is a familiar or unfamiliar sensation.
- Are you aware of times when you are more or less grounded?
- How grounded are you when you are:
  - At work, school, in nature, playing sports, relaxing.
- Take as long as you need to explore your ability to be grounded.
- When you feel complete, take a deep breath and open your eyes.

Some words people use to describe grounding include *calm*, *peaceful*, *protected*, *safe*, *secure*, *present*, *focused*, *heavy*, *confident*, *connected*, *aware*, and *strong*. Practice grounding every day. Grounding provides a foundation for your spiritual growth and intuitive development, no matter which ability or chakra you are focused on. You can use your grounding cord to release limits to accessing, activating and using your Intuition.

GROUNDING TO RELEASE ENERGY MEDITATION

Being consciously present within your body is the best way to take charge of your life, master your energy system, and access all of your intuitive abilities. Grounding is an important tool that we will make use of in all of the exercises in this book. You can also use grounding to release unwanted energy such as physical pain, emotional turmoil, mental anguish, self-limiting beliefs, other people's information, foreign energy, judgments, expectations, and unhelpful life circumstances. This meditation will help you to do this.

- Sit comfortably with your feet on the ground, a straight back, and your hands in your lap.

- Take a deep breath in and out, and continue a slow steady breath throughout your meditation.
- Be aware of your first chakra, which is an energy center near the base of your spine.
- Visualize an energy connection from there to the center of the planet.
- Allow the energy to flow through the chair, floor, Earth, and all physical matter.
- Be aware of the energy flowing from you to the center of the Earth.
- Imagine it is like a powerful laser, or a waterfall effortlessly cascading and flowing away.
- Take a moment to scan your body and notice if you are experiencing any discomfort.
- Notice if you are tense, anxious, or stressed out, or in physical, emotional, or mental pain.
- Release these unwanted energies down your grounding cord.
- Choose one at a time to focus on and feel yourself relaxing as you let them go.
- If you notice yourself resisting, simply send your resistance down your grounding.
- Focus on this exercise for as long as you wish.
- When you feel complete, take a deep breath and open your eyes.

GROUNDING ON A NATURE WALK MEDITATION

When you first learn the grounding technique, you may need to concentrate on it during your meditation time. The more you practice, the easier it will be, and the more you will feel the benefits. Eventually, you will be able to remain grounded when you are out and about in the world. You will be grounded at the supermarket, while you are driving, taking care of the kids, and at work even when you are busy.

Many people feel naturally grounded when in nature. This is because plants, animals, rocks, and soil are always in present time. By spending time in nature, you are invited to match the stillness and presence of Gaia. By being away from the madding crowd of humans, whose energy can be all over the place, you get to re-energize and regroup your own unique vibration. Next time you are out in nature, practice your grounding.

- As you walk in nature, be aware of your first chakra.
- Create an energy connection from there to the center of the planet.
- Allow the energy to flow through the ground and all physical matter.
- Relax and enjoy your walk while also being grounded.
  - Notice how your body responds.
  - Be aware if your walk is different because you are grounded.
- Allow your own unique experience.

Grounding and Intuition

Grounding from your first chakra is a great tool for enhancing your intuition. You can use your grounding to increase your sensitivity by using it to clear doubt and limits. You can remove interference from your energy field so your intuition gets clearer. You can cleanse your chakras by releasing unwanted energies that are stored in them during your grounding.

There are some other reasons why grounding is the most important technique you can ever learn. Spirit communicates through intuition. You are spirit and grounding ensures your intuition is relevant to this time-space reality. You can see and know things outside the body. But grounding makes your intuition real for the temporal self. Space is created in your energy field as you let go of foreign energy. You need to occupy that space or lose yourself and your access to your guidance. Grounding helps to do this because it makes it safe for your high energy to flow through your body. As you clear blocks you raise your vibration, you close the frequency gap between you and your body. By being more present in your body, you begin to take charge of this reality as spirit. You can feel, see, know, and hear as spirit inside the human experience. Your intuition development accelerates because you are focused in the here and now.

Some people find that listening to a recording helps them have a deeper experience. You can access a recording of the grounding technique and the other techniques taught in this book here: https://drlesleyphillips.com/intu-ition-and-chakras-readers-gift/.

Chapter 17
MEDITATIONS TO
TAKE CHARGE

You cannot master your life purpose, chakras, and intuition unless you are sitting in the driver's seat of your life. Your driver's seat provides the best perspective on what is going on around you. It places you at the controls of your vehicle (body) and gives you access to the console containing your guidance system (intuitive faculties). This chapter provides guidance on how to consciously center your higher consciousness within your physical body so you can steer the ship of your life.

You may think you are steering your life, but it is quite possible that you are not. Many humans are actually governed by the body's animal nature, or by other people's influences. The emotions, intellect, sex drive, and ego are powerful aspects of the physical body that can dominate your perception of reality. If you have strong emotional reactions to people and situations, where you are pulled in and swept away by them, or if the people around you are emotional and you trigger each other until the situation spirals out of control, then you are governed by your emotions.

When the going gets tough, you find yourself reaching for the candy, lighting a cigarette, grabbing a bottle from the liquor cabinet; opening your little black book and speed dialing your lover; pulling that copy of *Fifty Shades of Grey* from the shelf and escaping for a while; or all of the above. Then you may not be as in charge of your reality as you think you are.

If your mind can't stop thinking and you constantly worry about the future or obsess about the past; if you analyze everything, go round in circles weighing up pros and cons, until you are overwhelmed and still unable to decide, then you have a tendency to get caught in your intellect. The thinking brain is powerful but can run away with itself if spirit doesn't take charge. We are trained to be analytical. While the intellect is the highest capability of the body, it can block your intuitive abilities.

These examples show how we can allow the appetites of the body to take charge. The intellect, emotions, and sexuality are body energies. They can be so strong that we become completely absorbed by them. They can also be ways of abandoning the body and leaving it to fend for itself. It is like turning on the auto-pilot while you sleep at the wheel. You are spirit. Your body is your vehicle. While it is very capable, it isn't meant to run the show alone. The body's needs are important, but if no one is directing the show, it can be a farce when you wanted an opera.

Centering Technique

You, the spiritual being, have a very high vibration. Your body, which is made of dense matter, has a much lower vibration. Grounding makes it easier for you to occupy the body. Centering shows you where to seat your consciousness within your body. Playing with your big toe can be fun, but it might not be the most effective seat for playing master of your universe. A useful analogy to explain centering is to compare your life to an airport. Experiences come and go like airplanes and travelers. Some are in the distance, others are taxiing to the terminal, some are circling overhead. If you could be the air traffic controller, you could calmly direct them all from a neutral perspective to ensure safe landings and takeoffs. There is a seat for the soul within your body that allows you to do exactly that, and it is called the center of your head.

You are spirit. You are not your physical body. Your body is a vehicle for you, the spiritual consciousness. Yet as we have seen, the body has a mind of its own and unless you are in charge it will run the show. The secret to taking charge of it is by applying an ancient practice used by spiritual masters through the ages. It is the answer to maintaining a spiritual perspective while living in a physical body.

There is a small gland shaped like a pine cone in the center of your head. It is about the size of a pea and sits in between the two hemispheres of the brain at the top of the brain stem. It is located in a groove where the two halves of the thalamus join. This is the location of one of the seats of the soul within the human being. It was known about in ancient mystery schools.

In fact, the pine cone is a common motif in temple architecture from ancient Greece, Rome, Mesopotamia, and India. The ancient Egyptian symbol, the eye of Horus, is said to be a diagram of the pineal gland and thalamus. In ancient Taoist philosophy and Celtic myth, this same structure is called the Crystal Palace. In modern times, we call it the third eye. While some ancient cultures used to drill a hole in the skull as an activation ritual for the third eye, a preferable practice is to do it through focus, intention, and meditation.

CENTERING MEDITATION

Centering[34] allows your consciousness to take charge. It puts you in a place where you are above the emotions, and set apart from your intellect and worries. It also focuses you in present time as it seats you within your body. Being centered launches you on your journey to consciously activate your intuitive abilities as it ensures you can deal with the incoming information about yourself and others from a neutral, nonjudgmental perspective. The center of your head is where you can reside in the physical body. It is one of the seats of the soul taught in ancient mystery teachings. The center of your head technique helps you be neutral and in charge of your life.

- Sit comfortably with your feet on the ground, a straight back, and your hands in your lap.
- Take a deep breath in and out, and continue a slow steady breath throughout your meditation.
- Ensure you take the time you need to get grounded (see previous chapter).
- Focus your awareness above the top of your head.
- Enter your body through the top of your head.
- Settle in the center of your head.

34. Technique first learned from Flora, Mary Ellen. *Meditation*.

- Place your awareness here and relax.
- Experience this place.
- Take your time to get familiar with it.
- Move above your head and experience this.
- Move back to the center of your head, and notice the difference.
  - Experience what being in the center of your head is like.
  - Is it busy or calm; is it empty, clear, or fuzzy?
- Think of a word or phrase to describe it.
- Allow yourself to become aware of your consciousness.
- You might even see it as a bright spark of light.
- Take a deep breath, open your eyes.

If you had difficulty finding the center of your head, take your two index fingers. Place one in the center of your forehead, and the other above and behind one of your ears. Imagine a line of light emanating from each fingertip. The center of your head is where they intersect.

Practice centering every day, especially while doing the exercises in this book. Centering stimulates your sixth chakra and its intuitive abilities. By activating your sixth chakra, you develop your neutrality. When you start to see yourself clearly, you can accept whatever you have created without judging it. If you use your abilities to read others, you will be able to do the same for them. Centering can assist you to be neutral about your spiritual growth, intuition development, and other life challenges, such as physical pain, emotional turmoil, mental anguish, self-limiting beliefs, other people's information, foreign energy, judgments, expectations, and unhelpful life circumstances.

MEDITATION TO INCREASE CLARITY

In this meditation, you are going to increase your clarity by healing your pineal gland. This should make it easier for you to access your clairvoyance.

- Sit comfortably with your feet on the ground, a straight back, and your hands in your lap.

- Take a deep breath in and out, and continue a slow steady breath throughout your meditation.

- Take time to get grounded and centered (see the previous chapter).

- Relax and experience being in the center of your head.
    - Notice what the center of your head feels like right now.
    - Does it feel clear or cloudy; heavy or light, for example.

- You will now give the center of your head a healing.

- Release any unwanted energy from the center of your head down your grounding cord.
    - Let your mind fog drop away.
    - Release other people's energy.
    - Let go of pain, stress, or tension.
    - Remove any other distractions or disturbances.
    - Remove calcification from your pineal gland by sending it down your grounding cord.

- Sit in the center of your head and enjoy being the God of your own universe.
    - Notice if you now have a greater sense of clarity.

READING ENERGY MEDITATION

In this exercise, you will use your clairvoyance to sense your grounding cord and give yourself an intuitive reading about your energy, so that you can begin to validate your ability to operate consciously as spirit.

- Sit comfortably with your feet on the ground, a straight back, and your hands in your lap.

- Take a deep breath in and out, and continue a slow steady breath throughout your meditation.

- Take time to get grounded and centered (see previous chapter).

- Relax and experience being grounded and in the center of your head.
- From the center of your head, observe your grounding cord.
- Notice what it looks like.
  - What color is it?
  - Is the energy clear or dark?
  - Is it a weak or strong flow?
  - Are you aware of what you are releasing?
- Increase the flow of energy down your grounding cord.
  - Do this with your intention.
  - Continue until you are as grounded as you can be right here, right now.
- Release unwanted energy down your grounding cord.
- Observe your grounding cord to see if it changes as you release energy.
- Observe how it is changing.
  - What color is it now?
  - Is the energy clearer?
  - Is it a stronger flow?
  - What are you releasing now?

Centering and Science

Scientists have found structures like those present in the eyes inside the pineal gland. It has a lens, cornea, retina, and light-sensitive internal structures similar to the rods and cones in the eyes. It also produces melatonin and Di-methyl-tryptamine (DMT). Rick Strassman, author of the *Spirit Molecule*, believes this chemical plays a role in inducing mystical states of consciousness and is postulated to be produced at birth, death, during meditation, transcendent. and psychic experiences.[35]

The pineal gland also produces melatonin in the absence of light and during sleep. This hormone regulates skin color and body temperature,

---

35. Strassman, Rick. *DMT: The Spirit Molecule: A Doctor's Revolutionary Research into the Biology of Near-Death and Mystical Experiences.* Paris: Park Street Press, 2000.

governs circadian rhythms, eliminates free radicals, and is involved in cell repair. When you meditate, your brainwaves shift. According to Strassman, the pineal vibrates at these altered brain frequencies triggering DMT release. The pineal glands of many people are calcified and do not function correctly. Avoiding fluoride, mercury, and processed foods and drinking filtered water can help prevent this.

Centering and Intuition

Centering puts you in charge of your reality. When you center, you sit in the driver's seat of your life. You are above the emotional rollercoaster, disentangled from your monkey mind, and apart from the limits of your intellect. You can sit in the eye of the storm rather than be tossed on the tumultuous seas of life.

Centering focuses you in present time because it seats you in the body. It bestows acceptance and neutrality, which are invaluable qualities in your self-exploration. If you want to assist others through readings and healings, centering helps you view their reality without judging or having preconceived ideas about who they are or what they ought to do.

Centering stimulates your pineal gland, one of the seats of the soul in the physical body. The pineal gland is the narrow gate used to enter the kingdom of heaven that Jesus spoke of. It is the crystal palace of druid and Celtic folklore and the third eye of the ancient mysteries. By centering your consciousness in this pea-sized gland, you get access to the glorious gifts of spirit.

Centering places your consciousness at a window where you can view your reality from the perspective of spirit. It places you at a crucial interface with your brain and physical body. You can direct your life from here. You can bring spiritual information to guide your temporal self and creations. Once activated, the pineal gland allows you to view the spirit realm. You activate it by centering and bringing your light to it. Once it is activated you can see auras, chakras, thought forms, energy beings, memories, symbols, and much more.

Chapter 18
MEDITATIONS TO CREATE REALITY

Most people create by default. With intuition, you can create on purpose because it confers self-awareness. You can become aware of what you created and why. You can see how you created the reality you are in now. Then you can construct and deconstruct your life by sculpting what you want from the clay of what you don't. This chapter provides a perspective on how you may be creating your life unconsciously and how to do it consciously. We create our reality through our energy. If your energy field contains unhealed emotional constructs and thought forms, you will create your reality through them, until you remove them.

We have emotional patterns we get stuck in. Here are some examples:

- When my husband shouts, I freeze like I did when my dad scolded me as a child.
- If I don't get my way I sulk or have a tantrum like a toddler to get people to do what I want.
- Even though I am attracted to you, I snub you as I am afraid of my sexuality.
- When I want something from you I am delightful until I get it. Then I drop you like a hot potato.
- When you're getting attention I feel jealous and try to turn the attention on me.

Your emotions are energy impulses that radiate from you like a beacon in a lighthouse. They are vibrations that give the universe information about you. The universe responds by sending experiences that resonate with your signals. If you have ever asked why you keep creating the same experiences over and over again, or why you always attract the same kind of relationships, it is because of these signals. You are not a deliberate creator. You are an unconscious creator. You invite these experiences by being a vibrational match to them, and you will perpetuate them until you discharge your emotional patterns and change your vibration.

Not only do emotions broadcast your requests for the reality you create, but your thoughts do too. If you believe your daydreams are figments of imagination that never amount to much, think again. They are not puffs of smoke that dissolve when you focus on something else. If you reckon your private thoughts are innocent meanderings that can do no harm, like clouds floating on the ether, forgotten forever so long as you don't enact them, think again. Thoughts have energy and power. They are like rockets with a trajectory and momentum. Your thoughts send ripples through the fabric of the universe like a signal from a radio tower.

Whether you spend your days thinking about seeking vengeance, sex, peace, or love, you signal your interest in these things to the rest of the universe. The universe wants to match you up with what you are most interested in, so you will create more of what you think about. This can lead to creations you do not want, not only in life but also in other existences. Your intuition helps you observe your thoughts and change them. Then you can be a conscious thinker of deliberate thoughts to guide your life in a direction you prefer.

By focusing on body-spirit communication, you can attain emotional balance and a calm mind. Then you are no longer confined to behavior patterns created in your childhood. You can let go of the old life and masterfully bring in the new, improved version.

Creating and Destroying Technique

Energy is never destroyed but it is constantly moving and changing form. Because energy follows your thoughts, desires, and intentions, you can learn to consciously transform the energy within you and release it from your space. Being a master creator is the same as being a master destroyer. A lot of people get excited about manifestation and creating new things but have a problem letting go. If you don't let go of your old creations from your energy field, there may not be space for the new ones. While you are infinite, your body and your life are not; they are finite containers of experience.

Shopping for clothes is a great analogy to help explain this. If you buy new clothes every season and put them in your closet, you will eventually run out of space. You won't be able to see what you have, let alone create a matching outfit. But if you regularly sort through your closet and discard what you no longer wear, you have plenty of room for new items and can play with matching your outfits.

Creating and destroying is a spiritual principle that involves cleaning out your metaphorical closet. It is about giving yourself a spring clean by clearing old beliefs, thought patterns, and stuck emotions to make way for new ones. This frees up energy for new creations, like recycling your old clothes by donating them to charity. Your external environment is a reflection of your inner environment. If your closet is so stuffed full you can't see what you have, your life will reflect that state of being.

To flow easily through your life and create everything you want, it is helpful to have space for new creations. You can do this by letting go of old creations. Otherwise, you will feel stuck and your creative flow will be clogged. Later in this chapter, you will learn a technique for releasing what you no longer want in your life to make way for what you do. First, let's take stock of what you have created so far and how satisfied you are with it.

LIFE SATISFACTION EXERCISE

Rank the following eight areas of your life from 1 to 10, where 1 is a low satisfaction level and 10 is a high satisfaction level. Do it quickly and intuitively, don't think about it; your thoughts are not your intuition. Be honest; no one else will see this.

- Career, Work, Business
- Abundance, Finance, Money
- Health and Wellness

- Family and Friends
- Love and Romance
- Personal Growth
- Physical Environment
- Fun and Recreation

Once you have done this, pause, take some deep breaths, and get grounded and centered. Reflect on which areas are most and least fulfilled, and validate your ability to manifest in each one. You have created content and experiences in all of them.

Next, focus on each area and feel into its vibration. Ask if your intuition is guiding you to create change or let go. Use the neutrality of the center of your head technique (see the Centering Meditation in Chapter 17) to give you clarity. Use the healing power of the grounding technique (see Chapter 16) to release resistance to receiving your answers.

Once complete, congratulate yourself on being able to learn from life. Celebrate your ability to use intuition to be self-aware. You experienced your intuition if you came up with numbers instantly without making excuses or justifications; if you felt the vibration of each area and knew, saw, or heard your information about it; or if you received guidance about the changes you wish to create.

Validate how wise you are. You are a spark of divinity. Your information is in reach, can reveal your purpose, and lead you on your true path. Acting on your intuition is the best way to ensure you easily fulfill your destiny. In your notebook, make a list of your creations in each area. Place a note beside each item as to whether you still want this creation. Then make another list for what new creations you want to make.

CREATING AND DESTROYING MEDITATION

This meditation will teach you how to consciously create and let go using thought forms.

- Sit comfortably with your feet on the ground, a straight back, and your hands in your lap.

- Take a deep breath in and out, and continue a slow steady breath throughout your meditation.
- Take time to get grounded and centered.
- Relax and experience being grounded and in the center of your head.
- Create the mental image picture of a rose six to eight inches in front of your forehead.
- You may see the rose or just simply know it is there.
- Take time to admire your creation.
  - What color is it?
  - Is it a bud or full bloom?
  - What are the other distinguishing features?
  - Notice as many details about the rose as you can.

Congratulations, you consciously manipulated energy to create a rose. If you saw the rose, you were using your clairvoyance. If you knew it was there, you used your claircognizance. Now, you could leave it there, but if you did that it might interfere with you noticing other things, just like in the closet analogy. Therefore, you are now going to learn how to consciously destroy a thought form by practicing using roses.

- Now destroy the rose, let it go, let it disappear.
- You can do this by:
  - Allowing it to dissolve.
  - Exploding it like a firecracker.
  - Blowing it up.
  - Letting it fade away.
  - Allowing the wind to blow it away.
  - Chopping it into pieces and scattering it.
- Decide which way worked best for you.
- Then let all your roses go using this visualization.
- Practice this technique until you are comfortable with it.
- When you feel complete, take a deep breath and open your eyes.

Practice creating and destroying roses until you feel comfortable with this technique. Some people find this easy but others get caught in doubt and expectations. If this is you, simply release your doubt, expectations, frustration, or tendency to intellectualize down your grounding cord. You're getting used to working as spirit instead of body consciousness. It takes time to retrain the mind to let spirit take charge.

Sensing the Energy of Your Creations

When you are grounded, centered, and working with roses, you operate consciously as spirit. A great way to validate what you are doing is to feel the energy of the roses.

SENSING ENERGY IN ROSES MEDITATION

This exercise will allow you to validate that you really are consciously working with energy. You will get to experience the energy of your creation directly.

- Sit comfortably with your feet on the ground, a straight back, and your hands in your lap.
- Take a deep breath in and out, and continue a slow steady breath throughout your meditation.
- Take time to get grounded and centered.
- Create and destroy a few roses and admire your creations.
- Next create a rose in front of you and leave it there.
- Now lift your hand up to the rose and feel the energy.
- Destroy the rose and see if you can feel a difference.
- Keep your hand there to feel the energy while you create and destroy a few roses.
- Validate your ability to experience and manipulate energy.

RELEASING ENERGY IN ROSES MEDITATION

These roses are very powerful. You can even fill them with the energy of what you don't want and use the roses to release it. This works when you know what you want to let go of and when you don't. For example, "I am letting go of my fear of cats that stems from when I was scratched as a child" or "I am letting go of what prevents me from taking my next step."

- Sit comfortably with your feet on the ground, a straight back, and your hands in your lap.
- Take a deep breath in and out, and continue a slow steady breath throughout your meditation.
- Take time to get grounded and centered.
- Create a rose in front of you and admire your creation.
- Be aware of something you would like to let go of.
- Allow that energy to flow into the rose.
- Once the energy is in the rose, explode the rose.
- Repeat this to continue releasing unwanted energies.
- Do this for as long as you wish.

You can use the spiritual technique of creating and destroying to let go of anything. You can heal yourself by releasing stuck emotions and old emotional patterns. You can change your emotional set point by creating roses to move up the emotional scale from bad- to better-feeling emotions. You can release nonsupportive thought patterns and limiting beliefs. You can catch yourself with an unhelpful thought and put it in a rose before it gains momentum.

You can release concepts that no longer work for you as well as other people's energy that has influenced you, so it is easier to get in touch with your information. You can let go of other people's opinions, and strengthen and follow your inner voice. When using this technique, you might get a sense that even though you exploded a single rose, you need to do more. If that is the case, use multiple roses for the same block until you notice a shift in your energy. You may sense a void or empty feeling once the block has been released. Or if you can see the energy in the rose, you will see when it is empty or there is no more to pour into it. The more you practice, the more this technique will be second nature.

ROSES AND INTUITION MEDITATION

Now you will practice your clairvoyance and translate what you see into information that your brain can understand. You can do this simple rose reading every day to see yourself as spirit and keep track of your spiritual growth. Once again, validate your ability to operate consciously as spirit and use your intuition.

- Sit comfortably with your feet on the ground, a straight back, and your hands in your lap.
- Take a deep breath in and out, and continue a slow steady breath throughout your meditation.
- Take time to get grounded and centered.
- Create the mental image of a rose six to eight inches in front of you.
- Let this rose represent you as you are right here, right now.
- From the center of your head, be aware of its features
  - What color is it?
  - How open is it?
  - Translate the color into words.
  - What does this tell you about your spiritual growth?
  - What does this tell you about your current state of being?
- Take as long as you need until you have validated your current state of being.

Changing Your Reality

Creating and destroying is normal on this planet. Things are created and destroyed to give way for new things. The planet forms lakes and rivers that over time change landscapes. It makes volcanoes, earthquakes, and forest fires, which allow renewal. It creates seasons: spring, summer, autumn, winter. Every living thing on Earth is born, grows, and dies. You experience babyhood, childhood, being a teenager, adult, and senior. Finally, your body will experience death. The fact that nothing is permanent and everything is impermanent is useful information. If you get in a situation you don't like, you can relax as things will be sure to change. Learning how to consciously create and destroy makes you the master of your destiny.

CLEARING OLD ENERGIES EXERCISE

If you have resisted clearing your energy closet, you can use roses to do so now. A great place to start is by examining your old dreams to see if they are still what you want. Review your list of life passions and childhood dreams from Chapter 2. Notice if other people or your life experience made you believe they were not possible. Write about what you dreamed of being or doing before these influences. Note how much of what you truly wanted has manifested, as well as whether you still want these things.

You create your reality. This happens whether you are conscious of it or not. If you noticed that you have created a life that feels inauthentic, you can use creating and exploding roses to bring you back to your core. You may have fallen asleep because you focused on others or were programmed by culture. That's okay—you are waking up now! Take what you learned from doing this exercise and start to be a conscious creator.

As you use this technique to clear away your blocks, you can get clear on your life's big questions, such as what you came here for, the deepest yearning of your soul, and your deepest wishes and desires. You may think you know, but take a moment to take stock. Look at what you've created so far and ask how much is desirable versus undesirable, and which are your creations versus someone else's.

Having What You Want

Your intuition is a tool for guiding your life. Acting on it means allowing yourself to have what you truly want instead of choosing what you falsely believe you should want or what others want for you.

SELF-REFLECTION MEDITATION

This exercise helps you understand where you are on the scale of having what you want.

- Sit comfortably with your feet on the ground, a straight back, and your hands in your lap.
- Take a deep breath in and out, and continue a slow steady breath throughout your meditation.
- Take time to get grounded and centered.
- Imagine a scale from 0 to 100 percent.
- Use the scale to take the following readings:
    - The percentage you are in resistance versus allowing life to flow.
    - The percentage you allow yourself to receive compared to how much you deny yourself.
    - The percentage you let yourself have what you want.
- Think of a time when you knew what you wanted and you let yourself have it.
    - How did it feel?
- Now think of a time when you knew what you wanted and didn't let yourself have it.
    - How did that feel?
    - Did your body feel different this time?
    - What was the vibration of each experience?

Hopefully, you now see the difference that following your guidance can make in your life. When you experience desire, this is your affinity in guiding you in alignment with your highest good. If you ignore it in favor of what someone or something outside yourself wants, you will end up with something else. Use creating and exploding roses to release limits to having what you want.

DISCOVER WHAT BLOCKS YOUR CREATIVITY MEDITATION

- Sit comfortably with your feet on the ground, a straight back, and your hands in your lap.
- Take a deep breath in and out, and continue a slow steady breath throughout your meditation.
- Take time to get grounded and centered.
- Tune in to something you want right now that you are not allowing yourself to have.
  - Why are you not giving this to yourself?
  - Who is influencing you and why?
  - What are you afraid of?
  - Who do you need to please?
  - What belief is in your way?
- Does this give you some insight into what prevents you from following your intuition?
- Use creating and exploding roses to release these blocks.

Roses and Intuition

The roses are training wheels for spiritual mastery. We live in a holographic multidimensional universe. Playing with the thought form of a rose can give you access to the energy and information of everything. You can use them to give healings by allowing the roses to represent one of your chakras, a person, or situation. You can read yourself, another person, or a situation by interpreting the energy in a rose used to represent them. Roses can help you make choices between one thing and another, as they can show you what's best. You can also use roses to tell the truth from a lie, protect you from unpleasant energies, and validate that you can see, know, and sense energy.

This simple technique holds within it the key to being the God of your own universe. You can use your roses to see your personal truth, create new things, and destroy old things. That means you can take charge of your reality and build a world around you that matches your personal preference and perspective. It means you can change anything you wish and cope with anything that arises. You can use roses to defend you from a psychic attack and as a spiritual greeting to those operating as spirit.

Chapter 19
MEDITATIONS TO
STAY IN BALANCE

You cannot align to your unique life purposes unless you are also oriented to the planet. You are a multidimensional eternal being, capable of being in any time, any place, anywhere. Grounding helps you be present in your body on Earth. By balancing your energy with your environment, you can better relate to your body and this planet. Running Earth energy helps you relate to the planet and can help you release limits, relieve stress, and clear unwanted energy.

Earth was created as an adventure playground for you to learn about free will so you could eventually choose your path to source. There are many adventures, although some feel serious rather than a fun game. The ancients saw Earth as a great mother. She was called World Mother (Pachamama) in the Andes, Gaia in ancient Greece, Terra in Rome, and Mother Nature by the Celts. These cultures all recognized her as being a life giver and nurturer as well as a powerful and changeable host. They learned from her natural cycles and emulated her in the way they lived life.

The Yin/Yang symbol of Eastern philosophy describes the opposite polarities of Earth. Its rotation conveys how everything is in flux, and things are always changing from one opposite to another. Everything on Earth has an opposite, and balance is constantly being sought. Things can be up then down, left then right. People are male or female. They experience things as positive or negative, and feel healthy or sick, stressed or relaxed. The Earth's energy is a balancing force flowing through all that exists on this planet, including you.

Like you, the planet goes through constant cycles of growth and change. We can see this in the weather, seasons, night and day, earthquakes, volcanoes, floods, tsunamis, and forest fires. Earth has an inbuilt system to stay in balance. It is a cooperative system of organisms and energies. If things get out of balance then something occurs to redress the balance. The notion of balancing opposites extends to all things on Earth.

- In biology, all organisms maintain balance within their bodies to support life. For human life, blood must be maintained at a pH level between 7.35 and 7.45 and a body temperature between 97.8 and 99 degrees Fahrenheit. This is called homeostasis.
- In ecology, fish eat algae in a pond. Their population grows. Then their stock diminishes as they deplete the food supply. They die off, letting the algae recover and the cycle to begin again.
- The same atoms are present at the start and end of a chemical reaction, though they are rearranged.
- In physics, an object is balanced when stationary as there is no net force, or any force at play is balanced by an opposing force.

In your life, if you work too hard you might redress the balance by resting. If you are too serious, you might seek more fun. If you give to others without receiving, you're giving and receiving out of balance. Life on Earth is like riding on a teeter-totter. Sometimes you are up and sometimes down. Every time the teeter-totter changes sides it passes through a point of balance. If you pay attention, you can hold the point of balance. In your life things are always changing too. Like the teeter-totter, sometimes you are up and sometimes you are down. Like the yin and yang, you contain opposites within you, such as happy or sad, courageous or scared, welcoming or aloof, compassionate or hateful.

Because you are always going through cycles of growth and change, learning new things can sometimes put you out of balance. During these times you want to get back in harmony. Take a moment to think about your current growth cycle. Write in your notebook what you are seeking to balance.

Here are some common examples we all experience from time to time: needing to lose weight, sleep more, eat better, working too hard, feeling stressed and needing to rest, being sick and needing to get well.

Earth Energy Technique

As a child I loved to sit under trees. I would place my spine against the trunk of an old English Oak then imagine the energy of Earth flowing in through my roots and the energy of the cosmos through my branches. It was great to circulate energy like I was a tree. It renewed and rejuvenated me. The trees reminded me how to connect with Gaia. Earth is like a mother to us. We are like fledglings that flew the nest and forgot to stay in touch.

Visit your Earth mother every once in a while to receive her wisdom and support. Being in nature can help you tune in to your intuition as it can bring you to a place of stillness and presence where your body relaxes, your emotions calm, and your mind empties. Staying connected with Earth, using spiritual techniques such as grounding and centering, and creating and destroying roses can all help you stay balanced as your spiritual evolvement accelerates.

EARTH ENERGY MEDITATION

Use this technique to tune in to Earth and her balancing energies whether there is a tree nearby or not.[36]

- Sit in a straight-back chair with your feet on the floor and hands in your lap.
- Breathe deeply, relax and be aware of your body.
- Take time to get grounded and centered.
- Create and destroy a few roses to get settled.
- Be aware of energy centers in the arches of your feet.
- Visualize them like they are shutters in a camera lens.
- Open the shutters so energy flows through the aperture.

---

36. First learned from Flora, Mary Ellen. *Meditation.*

- Allow the energy to flow up channels in your legs.
- Experience Earth energy flowing up your legs: in through the feet, ankles, calves, knees, thighs, all the way up to your first chakra.
- Let the energy flow down your grounding cord.
- Notice how it enhances the energy flow down your grounding cord.
- Be still and experience this loop of energy coming in the feet and out the grounding cord.

Consciously running Earth energy can assist you to balance all areas of your life. That means it can help you release all that is out of balance in your system and will replenish it with more harmonious frequencies. Running Earth energy also helps you be more present and more focused because the energy of the Earth is based in the here and now. Running Earth energy will accelerate your spiritual growth as it helps you deal with your personal growth cycles more efficiently by releasing the past, doubts, fears, foreign energy, and more. It also helps you raise your vibration as you release the denser energies that hold you back.

Run your Earth energy every day and when you do the exercises in this book. Use it to release limits to accessing, activating, and using your intuition as well as to balance, cleanse, and clear your system. If you are giving readings or healings to others about their earthly creations, running your Earth energy helps you come from a place of affinity for this reality and is also a protection that helps you clear their energy from your space. For more about Earth energy, I recommend *Earth Energy: The Spiritual Frontier*, by Mary Ellen Flora.[37]

RUNNING EARTH ENERGY
IN DIFFERENT PLACES MEDITATION

You can experience different vibrations of Earth energy when you travel to different locations. The energy of a gentle stream is different from a hot mineral spring, lake, river, or powerful waterfall. The energy of your garden is different from the beach, a mountain, or a field. The energy of Mount Shasta is not the

37. Flora, Mary Ellen. *Earth Energy: The Spiritual Frontier*. Everett: CDM Publications, 1996.

same as Kilimanjaro. Vesuvius is different from Kilauea. Table Mountain and Uluru have different energies and histories.

The energy in different parts of the world is distinctive. There are even energy hot spots where your energy would be challenged, accelerated, or pacified. Some of these planetary energy centers amplify the Earth energy, keep it moving and changing, and others nullify or make it feel chaotic. There are even Earth energy vortices where you can upload new information or be assisted in releasing energy. When visiting a location where you deposited energy in a past life, you can reabsorb it and use it in this life.

The energy of the humans living in a country also has an influence on how it feels to be there. By grounding and running Earth energy at the different places you visit, you exchange energy with the planet. It can be fun to meditate in nature, experience her flavors, and notice how they impact your energy field.

The next time you visit your favorite beauty spot or are on vacation in a different land, try this meditation:

- Sit with your feet on the Earth and hands in your lap.
- Breathe deeply, relax, and be aware of your body.
- Take time to get grounded and centered.
- Create and explode roses to get settled.
- Be aware of energy centers in the arches of your feet.
- Visualize them like they are flower buds.
- Watch as they open like flowers opening to the sun.
- Allow the energy to flow up channels in your legs.
- Experience Earth energy flowing up your legs, in through the feet, ankles, calves, knees, thighs, all the way up to your first chakra and down your grounding cord.
- Feel the energy of Earth in this location.
- Enjoy the energy flow, notice what it feels like.
- Say hello to Gaia and ask her to give you a healing.
- Relax as all your cares are washed away.
- Allow Earth to bring you into balance.

EARTH ENERGY AND INTUITION MEDITATION

Now you will practice using your intuition to read your Earth energy and translate what you see into meaning so you can get a clear picture of your relationship with Earth's energy today.

- Sit with your feet on the Earth and hands in your lap.
- Breathe deeply, relax, and be aware of your body.
- Take time to get grounded and centered.
- Create and explode roses to get settled.
- Run your Earth energy as instructed above.
- From the center of your head, observe your Earth energy.
- Use your clairvoyance to see what color it is
- Know its vibration using your claircognizance.
  - Translate the color or colors into words.
  - Notice what you are using this vibration for.
  - Appreciate what this tells you about your current state of being.
  - Be aware if the color changes anywhere along its path.
  - If so, notice what it is picking up to make it change.

EARTH ENERGY AND HEALING MEDITATION

- Sit with your feet on the Earth and hands in your lap.
- Breathe deeply, relax, and be aware of your body.
- Take time to get grounded and centered.
- Create and explode roses to get settled.
- Run your Earth energy as instructed above.
- From the center of your head, observe your Earth energy.
- Use your clairvoyance to see the energy flowing.
  - Be aware if the energy is flowing easily.
  - Identify any blocks or limits to its flow.
  - Receive information on the cause of the block.

• Create and explode roses to increase the flow of Earth energy and to clear any limits to its flow.

Use Different Earth Energy Vibrations

Earth is abundant and plentiful, and many variations of Earth energy are available to you to work with. Just a glimpse at the photographs in a *National Geographic* magazine is enough to see the vast array of minerals and plant life that make glorious frequency expressions all over Earth. You can learn to run different vibrations of Earth energy depending on your needs. You do not need to visit a specific location to do this. All you need to do is consciously direct the frequency of Earth energy that you take in through the feet chakras.

EARTH ENERGY VIBRATIONS MEDITATION

In this meditation, we use color to represent the different Earth energy variations, but you could also choose the energies of crystals, minerals, or organic matter.

• Sit with your feet on the Earth and hands in your lap.

• Breathe deeply, relax, and be aware of your body.

• Take time to get grounded and centered.

• Create and explode roses to get settled.

• Run your Earth energy as instructed above.

• From the center of your head, be aware of your feet chakras.

• Watch them spinning and observe what color they are.

• You can sense the color by seeing, knowing, or feeling it.

• Be aware of what that frequency is being used for.

• Now choose a different vibration of Earth energy.

• Simply use your conscious intent to run the color you choose.

  • You can run blue, green, yellow, orange, red, or any other color you wish.

• Notice how this vibration of Earth energy makes you feel.

• Be aware of how you are changing in response to this energy.

- Play around with different vibrations and notice the difference between them.
  - How does red feel compared to pink or gold?
  - How does blue feel versus purple or other colors?
- Relax and enjoy playing with the different vibrations of Earth energy.
- Validate your relationship with the planet and how you are deeply connected.

Earth Energy and Intuition

All physical manifestations on this planet are made of Earth energy. This includes your body, and the animal, plant, and mineral kingdoms. These Earthly creations are interconnected evolutionarily and energetically by a multidimensional grid. Your intuition keeps you in awareness of how the planet and humanity are changing.

You can talk to the spirit of Gaia and all life using intuition. Intuition and Earth energy can help you balance your body and stay in synch with the planet. You can experience different aspects of Earth such as the energy of the mountains, forests, and rivers as well as communicate with the Devas and guardians of nature. They can help you heal and grow and provide a unique perspective on life in our world.

There are different vibrations of Earth energy. Running them through your system can show you different ways of setting your own energy. Running the energy of a mountain might help you ground, whereas running the energy of a waterfall might help you release energy or go with the flow. Gaia is a master of change and balance. You can use Earth energy to help you make changes and to come back into balance.

Chapter 20
MEDITATIONS FOR COSMIC CONSCIOUSNESS

You are a multidimensional eternal being. Other aspects of your consciousness are creating in other realities, while your body personality (the temporal aspect of you that is reading this now) is creating on Earth plane reality. By learning to consciously run cosmic energy, you balance your energy with the larger cosmic consciousness. By orienting to the rest of the cosmos, you align your purpose with the greater whole.

Cosmic energy is the creative energy force of the cosmos. All things, including you and Earth, are made from it. Cosmic energy is the energy of everything. It includes the dense, slow vibrations seen in physical matter and the vibrations of ultraviolet and infrared light, microwaves, radio waves, X-rays, cosmic rays, and gamma rays. It can be experienced as light, sound, vibration, and color.

Science has studied the brain waves of people in meditation and discovered that each brainwave frequency relates to a different state of consciousness (see Table 6). Regular meditation actually changes your brain. Neurons in a meditator's brain send information more quickly. Areas of the brain associated with learning, memory processes, emotion regulation, and executive decision making get larger.[38]

---

38. Lazar, Sarah. How Meditation Can Reshape Our Brains. TEDxCambridge 2011. Retrieved from https://www.youtube.com/watch?v=m8rRzTtP7Tc. Accessed April 2019.

Brainwave	Frequency (Hz)	Consciousness State
Beta	13 to 30	Not meditating, awake, alert
Alpha	8 to 12	Light meditation, relaxation
Theta	4 to 8	Deep meditation, light sleep, awareness, creativity
Delta	< 4	Transcendental meditation, deep restorative, healing sleep
Gamma	25 to 100	Meditative bliss, love, heightened consciousness; insight, intuition

Table 6: Brainwaves and States of Consciousness

Consciously running different frequencies of cosmic energy in meditation assists you to rapidly enter a desired state of consciousness that can assist in your spiritual work—whether you wish to meditate to relax or stimulate intuition. You can run specific frequencies that assist you in attuning to your life purpose, using your intuitive abilities, giving healings or connecting with divine beings and your personal God. You can even consciously run different cosmic vibrations through your chakras to achieve different results. By consciously running different vibrations of cosmic energy through your system, you can heal yourself, assist others to heal, and create what you want.

Cosmic energy refers to all frequencies of energy. Physicists, astronomers, and cosmologists study cosmic energy frequencies. Scientists work within frequencies that can be measured. Those who meditate or give healings and intuitive readings also work with cosmic energy. There are no limits to the frequencies these lightworkers can access. Cosmic energy carries information. Just think about fiber-optic cables transmitting your favorite TV show, or sending a text message that is displayed as digital light on a phone the other side of the world. Science has validated that man is made of light. Every cell, organ, and system in your body transmits light. The function of your entire metabolism depends on light. Your cells and neurons communicate with one another using light.[39]

39. Popp, Fritz Albert. *Integrative Biophysics: Biophotonics*. New York: Springer, 2003.

Cosmic Energy Technique

Running cosmic energy helps you connect with the cosmic consciousness and modulate your frequency to have different experiences. Consciously running your cosmic energy will accelerate your spiritual growth. It helps you deal with the growth it stimulates by allowing you to release the past, doubts, fears, foreign energy, and more. It helps you raise your vibration as you let go of the denser energies that hold you back.

COSMIC ENERGY MEDITATION[40]

- Sit in a straight-back chair with your feet on the floor and hands in your lap.
- Breathe deeply in and out and relax.
- Get yourself grounded and centered.
- Start to create and explode roses.
- Run your Earth energy up your leg channels and down your grounding cord.
- Create a neutral ball of cosmic energy above your head.
- Simply intend it is so and it will be.
- Bring the cosmic energy in through the top of your head.
- Allow it to flow down through the back of your crown chakra.
- Let it flow down energy channels on either side of your spine.
- Let it flow down your back until it reaches your first chakra.
- When the cosmic energy reaches the first chakra, allow it to blend with the Earth energy.
- Bring this blended energy up through channels in the front of your body.
- Allow the energy to fountain out the top of your head.
- Let it flow around you through your energy field.
- Take a shower in all this wonderful cosmic energy.

---

40. First learned from Flora, Mary Ellen. *Meditation*.

- Allow some of the energy to branch off near the cleft of your throat.
- Let it flow through channels in your arms and out the palms of your hands.
- Be still and enjoy the energy flowing through your system.
- Practice this circuit several times.
- Let the Earth energy flow up your leg channels and down your grounding cord.
- Let the cosmic energy flow down your back and up your front channels.
- Allow it to branch off at the cleft of the throat and flow down your arm channels.
- Let the energy flow freely all around you. Experience and enjoy running energy.
- Be grounded and centered and have your Earth and cosmic energies flowing.

Run your cosmic energy every day. Run it when you are reading this book and practicing the exercises in it. Use your cosmic energy to release limits to accessing, activating, and using your Intuition Blueprint and to balance, cleanse, and clear your system. For more information about cosmic energy, I recommend *Cosmic Energy: The Creative Power* by Mary Ellen Flora.

COSMIC ENERGY AND INTUITION MEDITATION

We naturally use different cosmic energy vibrations to heal, process our experiences, create change, and alter the mood. You can practice your clairvoyance to read your Cosmic Energy and translate what you see into meaning so you can get a clear picture of your spiritual growth and relationship with the cosmos today.

- Sit in a straight-back chair with your feet on the floor and hands in your lap.
- Breathe deeply in and out and relax.
- Get yourself grounded and centered.

- Start to create and explode roses.
- Run your Earth energy up your leg channels and down your grounding cord.
- Run your cosmic energy down your back channels, and up your front channels.
- Let it branch off near the cleft of your throat, and flow down your arms and out your palms.
- From the center of your head, observe your cosmic energy.
- Use your clairvoyance to see what color it is.
    - Translate the color or colors into words.
    - Notice what you are using this vibration for.
    - Appreciate what this tells you about your current state of being.
    - Be aware if the color changes anywhere along its path.
    - If so, notice what it is picking up to make it change.

COSMIC ENERGY AND HEALING MEDITATION

- Sit in a straight-back chair with your feet on the floor and hands in your lap.
- Breathe deeply in and out and relax.
- Get yourself grounded and centered.
- Start to create and explode roses.
- Run your Earth energy up your leg channels and down your grounding cord.
- Run your cosmic energy down your back channels, and up your front channels.
- Let it branch off near the cleft of your throat, and flow down your arms and out your palms.
- From the center of your head, observe your cosmic energy.
- Use your clairvoyance to see the energy flowing.
- Sense how this cosmic energy is flowing.

- Be aware if the energy is flowing easily.
- Identify any blocks or limits to its flow.
- Receive information on the cause of the block.
- Create and explode roses to increase the flow of cosmic energy and to clear any limits to its flow.

Use Different Cosmic Energy Vibrations

Running cosmic energy allows you to consciously alter your vibration. This is useful in all aspects of your reality. You can raise or lower your vibration, increase your focus, heal yourself, have clearer communication or create whatever you want in material or spiritual form. You can run cosmic energy to be neutral, amused, or in any state you desire. You can vibrate with love, peacefulness, and enthusiasm. By learning to run different vibrations of cosmic energy during meditation, you can enter different states of consciousness.

MEDITATION TO SENSE COSMIC ENERGY VIBRATIONS

- Sit in a straight-back chair with your feet on the floor and hands in your lap.
- Breathe deeply in and out and relax.
- Get yourself grounded and centered.
- Start to create and explode roses.
- Run your Earth energy up your leg channels and down your grounding cord.
- Create a colored ball of cosmic energy over your head.
  - Choose whatever color you wish: red, orange, yellow, green, blue, violet, indigo, pink, gold, etc.
- Bring this cosmic energy frequency in through the top of your head.
- Let the cosmic energy flow down your back and up your front channels.
- Allow it to branch off at the cleft of the throat, and flow down your arm channels.
- Let the energy flow freely all around you. Bathe in this colored energy field.

- Be aware of your experience.
  - Explore whether your body enjoys this energy.
  - Find out how you feel running it.
  - Notice if it is creating any changes in your system.
- Change the vibration of cosmic energy you are running.
- Tune your awareness into this vibration.
  - Explore whether your body enjoys this energy.
  - Find out how you feel running it.
  - Notice if it is creating any changes in your system.
- Repeat this as many times as you wish.
- Play with cosmic energy to discover it for yourself.

Cosmic Energy and Intuition

Cosmic energy is the energy of everything. You are a multidimensional vibrational being. You create in this reality and many others. You can use different vibrations of cosmic energy to change your frequency and your reality. You can use it to be neutral, playful, serious, or any other way you wish to be. It can assist in your communication with your Trusted Source, and personal God, higher-self, angels, guides, and other beings of light. You can run different cosmic energy vibrations to modulate your frequency up and down and sideways. You can observe the vibrations of cosmic energy in your own space to learn about your spiritual growth. You can read the vibrations being used by others to understand them better.

Cosmic energy can be used consciously to stimulate change, improve health and well-being, and promote healing and recovery from illness. You can consciously run it through your auric field, energy channels, and chakras.

Chapter 21
KEEP YOUR INTUITION FLOWING

Congratulations, you have almost completed the book. You now understand how you have a unique spiritual communication system specially designed to guide you on your path and support your goals. Plus you have received a toolkit of meditation techniques to support your intuition development. In this chapter, you will document the unique profile of intuitive abilities you were born with and relate them to your life purpose. You will discover how to keep your intuition flowing and follow your intuition development plan.

Identify Your Intuition Blueprint

When people come to me for a Psychic Ability Blueprint,[41] I access their information from an altered state of consciousness, called a trance. This enables me to read their chakras and aura, access their Akashic Records, and communicate with their soul or higher self. You can learn to channel information from a trance state too. This involves mastery over your energy system and chakras. An appropriate preparation for this is to lay a strong foundation using the meditation techniques taught in this book. You will now explore your intuition using these techniques, and do some fun self-exploration exercises. You'll start

---

41. *Intuition Blueprint* is the process you are using in this book to discover your unique profile of intuitive gifts. *Psychic Ability Blueprint* refers to my process of accessing your information from your Akashic Record from the trance state. https://drlesleyphillips.com/psychic-abilities-blueprint/.

to identify your Intuition Blueprint by exploring your intuition experiences and challenges.

Refresh your memory on the types of intuition, outlined in Part Two, and then complete two exercises for each, described below.

YOUR INTUITION EXPERIENCES EXERCISE

Everyone has stories about intuition. Use the techniques you learned in Chapters 16 to 20 to enter a relaxed state. Ground, center, and run your energies. Then recall times when you used your intuition. Even if it isn't something you previously would have called intuition.

After the meditation, list your experiences in as much detail as possible. Next, identify which chakras and styles of intuition you used. Refer to chapters in Part Two to remind you about them. You may want to do several meditations, using the examples in those chapters to prompt your memory.

Take the time to recall as many incidences as you can. I suggest creating a table in your notebook with three columns. Describe your intuition experiences in the left column. Then put the relevant chakra in the middle column, and the form of intuition you used in the column next to that.

YOUR INTUITION CHALLENGES EXERCISE

Identifying how you block your intuition can also give you clues to your life purpose and unique profile of intuitive gifts. What appear to be our biggest challenges can become our greatest gifts when we overcome them.

At the end of Chapter 4, you identified your main life challenges. You related each challenge to a specific chakra. Turn to this page in your notebook. Many of the stories in Part Two describe people like you, who had struggled to overcome challenges in order to develop their gifts. Refer back to these stories and reflect on how you relate to them. Add any new examples you become aware of to your list.

After updating your list, use the techniques from the book to enter a relaxed state. Ground, center, create and explode roses, and run your Earth and cosmic energies. Choose a challenge from your list. Ask how it relates to your personal intuition style. You might be surprised at what emerges. Go through your list, and after meditating on each item, record the information you received. Refer to Table 1 in Chapter 1 to remind yourself of all the different intuitive abilities and their relationship to the chakras.

Create Your Intuition Chart

Take what you learned in the above exercises and use it to create Your Intuition Chart. The purpose of this exercise is to get to know yourself better and build awareness of your overall Intuition Blueprint. It doesn't matter if your experience has been positive or challenging. Either way, it indicates an area where you are focused as spirit.

YOUR INTUITION CHART EXERCISE

Create a copy of the chart found in Figure 2. Then transfer the number of intuition stories and challenges from the previous two exercises into the appropriate row and column. To get your final scores, add up the two numbers in each row to see where there is a concentration of experience.

Chakra	Ability	Experiences	Challenges	Total
First	Survival			
Second	Clairsentience			
Third	Energy Distribution			
	Astral Experience			
Fourth	Affinity			
	Oneness			
Fifth	Clairaudience			
	Inner Voice			
	Broad Band Telepathy			
	Narrow Band Telepathy			

Chakra	Ability	Experiences	Challenges	Total
	Pragmatic Intuition			
Sixth	Clairvoyance			
	Abstract Intuition			
Seventh	Trance Mediumship			
	Claircognizance			
Sixth, Seventh	Precognition			
H, 6, 7	Psychometry			
Hands 6, 7, 1	Healing			
	Telekinesis			

Figure 2: My Intuition Chart Example

Review the scores to see if it makes sense to you. For example, perhaps you have the potential to be a great communicator and your fifth chakra shows a strong focus. Or you are more sensitive to emotions and your clairsentience has a higher score. If you have a lot of challenges in an area, this tells you where you are in the spectrum of developing this ability and being clear about its messages. This is not a scientific assessment of your intuition, nor are your results set in stone; rather, they are pointers to help you explore yourself more deeply and make sense of your abilities as they exist today.

Review the entire chart to see if certain intuition styles stand out and if there is a pattern. As you explore your Intuition Blueprint, ask how it makes sense given what interests you, or what you feel passionate about. As you can see from your list of intuition stories and challenges, you've had clues about your intuitive gifts your whole life. If you are mainly following your life purpose free from influences that keep you out of alignment, you might have had more positive experiences. If you have been programed to follow some-one else's ideal for your life, then you might have had more challenges.

The chart points to your unique profile of intuitive gifts, which reflect what you are calling forth this lifetime. It is a starting point to further developing your intuitive abilities.[42] High or low scores don't mean you are good or bad at something. If you haven't experienced clairvoyance or other abilities, you can learn to. The path of the intuitive involves a meditation practice to turn within, self-healing to clear what gets in your way, and energy tools to help you access your information. When you are in a state of nonresistance, you are in alignment with your higher self and your intuitive abilities flow easily. If you are resisting your life in any way, the energy in your chakras can become blocked and so does your intuition.

What stops your intuition is twofold: first, there are things that get in your way, and second, nobody has taught you how to do it. You can use the meditation techniques presented in this book to release what blocks you, and to help you access your messages. I recommend you commit to a daily meditation regime and practice the techniques you have learned. The more you use them, the clearer you will be and your intuition will flow. It is also a good idea to decide which intuitive gifts you wish to develop further and make a plan to do so.

Your Daily Meditation Practice

You have learned how to use meditation to clear blocks, limiting beliefs, and other energies from your field. Be patient and take the time you need to clean your energy field. How much time you need will depend on your unique circumstances. The good news is you can clear it in less time than it took to accumulate, and there will be a tipping point when you will feel clearer than before. Each time you let something go, you raise your vibration, which makes it easier for you to access and validate your intuition.

Even when you pass the tipping point, you will still have new experiences to process and ongoing exposure to various energies and people. If you offer readings and healings, you might absorb your client's energy. Even if you don't, you still have family, friends, pets, news reports, shopping trips

---

42. For a complimentary quiz to identify your strongest "clair-ability," go to https://drlesley-phillips.com/psychic-abilities-quiz/.

to crowded supermarkets, and other ways to develop disturbances. You can stay on top of it by having a daily meditation practice. Think of it like cleaning your teeth or taking a shower. Do your energy hygiene with the same commitment as your physical hygiene because just as your body gets dirty, the following things can show up in your daily life: physical pain, emotional turmoil, mental anguish, foreign energy, self-limiting beliefs, other people's information, judgments, expectations, and unhelpful life circumstances.

Limiting energies may have been in your system since you were a single cell, embryo, baby, or even a past life. You don't yet know what it's like not to have them. You may feel very different once they're gone. It is important to clear these unwanted vibrations at a pace that is comfortable for your body. If you clear too many things at once, you may go into overwhelm. The meditation techniques are very powerful. When you use them, your growth will accelerate and your life will change because you are changing what is present in your energy field, and you create your reality as a reflection of what is in this field.

Pay attention to the shifts in your reality as you do this work. Changes that happen in your life are no coincidence. Changes you make as spirit using the techniques happen instantly because you are working outside of time and space. However, the body exists in time and space, and it will enter a growth cycle in response to what you have changed. Take a break and slow down if you need to. As you clear out limits, your body will respond and may need recovery time. Be sure to allow the integration time it needs.

You create your reality, and what you create depends on what is in your energy field. You change your energy field when you meditate, and your reality will change as a result. Once you start paying attention to what you stored in your body, it might start offering suggestions about what to clear next. It could draw attention to stored fear, anger, and pain precisely because now you are paying attention. Your growth could be experienced in a gentle or extreme way depending on your relationship with your body. Things will be much easier if you communicate with your body and remain grounded and centered as your growth unfolds.

Pay close attention to your body and its needs during this time. If you are not sure how to talk to your body, imagine it is your child. Tell it you love it. Reassure it that you are listening. Explain that the healing work you are doing is to help it feel better and you plan to take care of it throughout. Remember, as you change it needs to adjust. It might need more or less sleep, exercise, sex, or food. Or it might need a change of scene or a change of diet. Don't judge, give it what it needs, and it will support your growth.

It is possible to shift your entire reality in an instant. Those who experience this often spend years assembling a new sense of who they are and where they fit in the world. For most people, spiritual growth is gradual. You may need many meditations to clear all your blocks. Things you thought had gone might re-appear weeks or even years later. Don't get frustrated. You are making progress. It's just that sometimes there are multiple layers to get through. Use the meditation techniques to peel away the layers as they come up. Trust that divine timing is working to support your growth. When you use your new meditation techniques, you operate consciously as spirit and can identify and release the energies causing your problems.

MEDITATION TO CLEAR YOUR INTUITION BLOCKS

Now that you have learned all five techniques, you may use them to transcend your limits. You can use them to clear the seven major blocks to intuition covered in Chapter 5. Review your notes to remind yourself which of the intuition blocks you resonated with the most. Whether it was having a busy life, being unable to quiet your mind, being unable to calm your emotions, or approaching your intuition through effort, perfectionism, logic, doubt, or fear. You can use this meditation to shift these blocks and free yourself to act on your intuition.

- Sit in a straight-back chair with your feet on the floor and hands in your lap.
- Breathe deeply in and out. Remember this is your time to relax.
- Create your grounding cord and release distractions.
- Run your Earth energy up your leg channels and down your grounding cord.
- Run your cosmic energy down your back channels, and up your front channels.

- Let it branch off near the cleft of your throat, and flow down your arms and out your palms.
- Get yourself centered, so you can be:
  - above your emotions
  - apart from your noisy intellect
- Create and explode roses to release:
  - emotional overwhelm
  - your busy monkey mind
  - effort, so you can operate as spirit
  - perfectionism, so you can accept yourself exactly as you are
- Be aware of any way in which you doubt or fear your intuition.
- Allow the flow of energies to clear your doubt and fear.
- Release them down your grounding cord and by creating and exploding roses.
- Let go of all resistance to following your intuition down your grounding cord.

Give yourself permission to repeat this meditation often. Each time you do, it you will clear more limits. You will raise your vibration, and it will be progressively easier for you to access your intuition.

MEDITATION TO TRANSCEND YOUR LIMITS

In Chapter 5, you learned the three biggest reasons people resist their own guidance: being influenced by someone else, having low self-esteem, and having self-limiting beliefs. Then at the end of Chapter 6, you also became aware of some of your limiting beliefs and where or from whom they came from. You can now use your meditation techniques to transcend these limits, so you can turn the challenges you listed at the start of this chapter into strengths. You can even use them to clear out old creations and make way for new ones.

- Sit in a straight-back chair with your feet on the floor and hands in your lap.
- Breathe deeply in and out. Remember this is your time to relax.
- Create your grounding cord and release limits to using your intuition.
- Be in the center of your head and create and explode roses to release limits.
- Run your Earth energy up your leg channels and down your grounding cord.
- Run your cosmic energy down your back channels, and up your front channels.
- Let it branch off near the cleft of your throat, and flow down your arms and out your palms.
- Be aware of someone who influenced your beliefs about intuition.
- Release their energy down your grounding cord.
- Create and explode roses to let go of their limiting beliefs about you and your intuition.
- Keep going until you feel a shift in your energy and a sense of relief.
- Be aware of any way in which you limit yourself.
- Allow the flow of energies to clear your unworthiness.
- Release self-limiting beliefs down your grounding cord and by creating and exploding roses.
- Validate yourself. You are spirit, you are intuitive. You can create the reality you want.

Do this meditation often, choosing different influencers and limits to work on each time. The more foreign energy and information you clear, the easier it will be for you to connect with your own information. It is helpful to work on your parents, siblings, and spouse, as well as others who have been influential in your life.

Find Your Life Purpose

The more you meditate, the clearer you will become and the easier it will be for you to know who you are and why you are here. You will understand your purpose as a spark of divine consciousness to anchor light in this reality. You will know your unique vibration and gifts to humanity, and you will understand the purpose in each and every moment of your life, no matter how big or small.

Your Intuition Vision and Mission

There are many ways to be an intuitive. I know professionals who consciously use their intuition in many fields of endeavor, including a detective, policewoman, and lawyer. I have met teachers, scientists, nurses, doctors, pharmaceutical sales reps, as well as psychologists and counselors who rely on it as a foundation for their work. Most of my clients are professionals. I have helped CEOs and executives develop their gifts and improve their personal lives and businesses. I have also helped practicing healers and psychics enhance their abilities. You can use your intuitive gifts to make your life better too.

There are also many ways to be a healer. All comedians are healers as it is nearly impossible to feel ill when you are having a belly laugh. This is because laughter instantly raises your vibration above your concerns. Having a life purpose as a healer doesn't necessarily mean you are a doctor, nurse, healthcare practitioner, dietician, veterinarian, therapist, herbalist, yoga instructor, personal trainer, spiritual teacher, or energy healer; although it can. An environmentalist is a healer. So is a woman who shares her story of dealing with breast cancer to inspire recovery of others; a mother who soothes her child's scraped knee; a hairdresser who listens to her client's woes; and a car mechanic who greets his customers with a smile and makes them feel better about their broken car.

To affirm where you fit in terms of using your intuition, meditate on how you want to apply what you have learned in this book. Then you can be certain if you want to use it to be of service to others, in your work, or elsewhere in your life.

VISION AND MISSION MEDITATION

- Sit up straight, feet on the floor and hands in your lap.
- Breathe deeply in and out and relax.
- Start by grounding and centering.
- Run your Earth and cosmic energies.
- Create and explode roses to release doubt.
- Be in the center of your head.
- Visualize yourself in the future using your intuition.
  - Notice what you are doing.
  - Observe how you are using it.
  - Be aware how it fits into everyday life.
- Reflect on your life mission.
- Be aware of how your intuition fits this purpose.
  - Will you incorporate it into your career or business?
  - Are there specific projects you can apply it to?
- Continue in this meditation until you feel complete.
- Create and explode roses to adjust your energy and then open your eyes.

Perhaps you will find that you just want to use it in your daily life, personal meditation practices, or with friends and family. Or maybe you wish to be a professional intuitive or healer. Whatever you discovered, describe your vision and write about your mission in your notebook.

YOUR LIFE PURPOSE STORY EXERCISE

Now let us connect the dots between your Intuition Blueprint and your vision and mission.

Review the information you now have about your intuition and life purpose and look for connections and patterns. Consider how your Intuition Blueprint might help you fulfill your purpose. Write a summary about how your intuition was purpose-built to serve your unique life purpose.

To inspire you, read the stories at the end of Chapter 1 as well as the following additional stories from my practice's Psychic Ability Blueprint sessions.

Jenny's Purpose as an Inspired Motivator

Jenny Munford's Intuition Blueprint indicated a life purpose as an inspired motivator of humanity. When I met her, she was recovering from the dissolution of her once successful business. She learned many lessons about herself and others through this painful time, including how emotions can be a system for guidance or sabotage. She realized the importance of body-spirit communication for positive life experiences and developed her spiritual awareness and emotional intelligence. She had a vision of humanity as an awakened species and her purpose was as a motivator of collective human consciousness. She wanted to create structures that would serve us all. Her business experience was an exploration of these old fear and greed paradigms not working and this enabled her to embody a strong desire for change.

Jenny is a motivational force, here to inspire people to change by planting seeds of possibility. She has the potential to be a motivational speaker and broadcaster. Her chart showed her fifth chakra was blocked in childhood when her parents sought to contain their precocious child. She was an extrovert forced to be an introvert. Now she must clear this invalidation and reclaim her inner voice and ability to self-express. She was telepathic as a child, but turned it down when others couldn't hear her. By overcoming these blocks, she could unleash her ability to inspire others to step into their highest self-expression too.

Clarity from clairvoyance was a strength she used her whole life, but it made her feel different. She oscillated between being her bright self versus fitting in. She was relieved to hear she could be a beacon of light offering others a chance to shine too. As she spread seeds of awareness, some would grow the seed and others wouldn't, and that was okay. She could allow everyone space to be where they were. There was a belief that humans are self-destructive that held her back. As a master of manifestation, many of Jenny's life lessons related to creating and destroying. Her business had been her spiritual training wheels for embodying this information. Her life continues to be a process of being more embodied so she can inspire others. What she created so far is a fraction of what she is capable of. I have no doubt she will continue to heal and expand.

Becky Clears Karma to Fully Use Her Gifts

Becky Kimes is a gifted healer who has created her own healing modalities, assisted by star beings. She wondered why she wasn't yet creating an abundant healing practice. In her case, all the blocks came from past lives. Her purpose was to clear them, and be a successful healer and teacher. She had many past lives as a seer. Her abilities were amazing but limited due to imprisonment, ridicule, death, and torture in prior lives. Her life plan included overcoming a tendency to please others that made her override her intuition; misusing her power; being manipulated by others for their gain; being blamed when things didn't work out as others wanted; and fearing her intuition would get her into trouble.

She was working on setting healthy second chakra boundaries so she would no longer let responsibility for others override her needs. She knew her life plan included ministering to groups, but she was afraid this would overwhelm her so she held back on promoting her business. Yet the reading showed she could expand incrementally and adjust her energy in a stepwise fashion. She had lots of energy but had given it away. Now she was seeking a healthy balance. If she focused on herself and divine source, she could hold her own vibration, regardless of what others did. By letting them be where they were, she could rise above and serve as a beacon of light they could be attracted to when they were ready. In prior lives, she received information through prophetic dreams. This time, she wished to experience her gifts in an awakened state.

Becky's fifth chakra was her main growth area, where she was releasing karmic imprints of misuse of power, self-judgment, regrets, fear of being wrong, and mistrust of others, so she could help create a new Earth. Seniority with her inner voice would allow her own perspective, no matter what others said. By releasing a pattern of using telepathy to intuit what others wanted, she could apply it in teaching. Becky's clairvoyance and abstract intuition were powerful. She had used different symbolic systems in past lives, but pain and invalidation diminished her ownership of her sixth chakra in this life. She was working on reclaiming it in present time. She was releasing doubt that humans can change so she could fully express these gifts. The plan for her life was poised to manifest, and as she does her inner work, I'm sure she will actualize her dreams.

Karishma and the New Generation of Implementers

Karishma studied journalism but was working in a tech company. She felt a strong urge to write about women's empowerment. During our session, Mother Mary and Mother Teresa came through. They heard her call to be of service, and they were guiding her to fulfill this dream and help create a more balanced society. Karishma was amazed because she had been thinking about Mother Teresa all that week. As it turned out, she had a past life working with her.

As we delved into her life story, more emerged about her purpose. Initially, she was embedded in a reality where she could witness the disempowerment of women. This helped spark her passion. In childhood, she struggled to stay in her body due to seizures. This fight between body and spirit was caused by a shocking birth experience, which she healed by using her clairsentience and inner voice to open communication with her body. Then her trance mediumship and energy distribution focused her energy through her body. All that remained was to gain seniority over her intellect. Then she could channel new ideas using her knowingness and trance mediumship, and use her intellect to translate the information through her writing.

Karishma's fifth chakra was a major part of her growth. Her inner voice was helping her have and express her unique point of view. Her telepathy would help her ideas gain mass appeal and build group consensus on better ways of doing things. She wanted her ideas on women's empowerment to be inclusive and result in harmony. She is part of a new wave of light workers who are implementers of the new world. Many of the older light workers have felt alone, but Karishma would be part of a cohesive group. Her pragmatic intuition was helping her follow the breadcrumbs. Her clairvoyance was helping her have clarity about new ways of being and to clearly express these high vibration options. Her claircognizance was helping her receive ideas from lightening presences such as Mother Teresa and Mother Mary. They were helping her open her heart to imagine what our world would be like if it was governed by a mother's love.

Your Intuition Development Plan

Reading this book, and exploring your intuition, life purpose, challenges, and desires have already stimulated growth. Now is a good time to reflect on your journey and make a commitment to continue what you started. By following the exercises in this book, you are already well on your way to developing your own multidimensional communication system. By continuing to use the meditation techniques to clear your energy field and activate your chakras, your intuition will continue to develop. Here are some examples of what I mean:

- By practicing grounding, you, the high vibration being, can occupy your body.
- By centering, you stimulate your pineal gland and activate your clairvoyance.
- By sitting in your crown, you enter a state of being and receive your information.
- By creating and exploding roses, you become a master energy manipulator.
- If you see the roses, you see clairvoyantly.
- If you know the roses are there, you use your knowingness.
- By running your Earth and cosmic energies, you balance your energy and heal yourself.

The paths of the intuitive are varied, and developing each form of intuition offers many adventures. Regardless of your unique style, intuition can help you overcome challenges. Whether you wish to use it for yourself or to be of service, it can help you achieve everything you wish to be, do, and learn.

Your Next Steps for Intuition Development

Your personal Trusted Source will never abandon you and will always guide you. It will show you each step on your path to a life of consciousness and purpose. All your angels and guides are aspects of divine consciousness. They are always available to support you. You can talk to your higher powers through your intuition. One of the best ways to communicate with your higher self and Trusted Source is through your claircognizance. This sense of knowingness is located in your crown chakra. Enter the experience of knowing by placing some of your consciousness in the crown. The following short meditation will help you receive answers from your Trusted Source about your next steps in developing your intuitive senses.

INTUITION NEXT STEPS MEDITATION

- Sit up straight, feet on the floor and hands in your lap.
- Breathe deeply in and out and relax.
- Ground, center and run your Earth and cosmic energies.
- Create and explode roses to cleanse your energy.
- Move your consciousness to the crown of your head.
- Be still and know yourself as spirit.
  - Know yourself.
  - Know your Trusted Source.
  - Know yourself as an aspect of divine consciousness.
- Be still and know your best next steps.
  - Are there meditations you want to do regularly?
  - Is there a friend you can practice with?
  - Do you want to take some courses?
- Be in your crown chakra.
- Ask any question you wish and know the answer.
- Ask another question and effortlessly receive your information.
- Ask questions until you feel complete.
- Create and explode roses to adjust your energy.

Once you have finished meditating, write down everything you became aware of. See if you can formulate them into a series of goals.

Find a Great Intuition Teacher

Everyone is unique. Your intuition profile is completely different from everyone else's. Your purpose is special to you. You can let it unfold naturally, and you can consciously direct it. A good teacher will use their intuition to help light your way so you do not stumble in the dark. They will keep you accountable so you do not go back to sleep or fall into the traps of your own ego. Spiritual growth is happening always, but it can happen on purpose, and more quickly and easily with an experienced teacher helping you.

Each awakening human forges a unique path of spiritual evolvement. You will explore your chakras like no one else will. There is no particular order you are meant to open them. There is just the way it happens for you. A good teacher recognizes this and will validate that every experience you have is an opportunity to learn.

There are many spiritual systems to choose from to awaken your intuition. The tools presented in this book are ancient. If you choose to use them, they will give you a solid foundation on your path to spiritual awakening. They seem simple and they are, but they work on a multidimensional level and you can do a lot more with them than given so far.

While it is possible for you to unlock your intuition on your own, there is no substitute for a good teacher. The best intuition teachers are those who recognize your uniqueness and help you remember your greatness. They can help you to be honest about where you are in your growth as well as guide you from their wisdom and experience. The "About the Author" section has some information on how to proceed if you would like to work with me. Whatever you choose, remember you can't ever get it wrong, though you can make it easier.

If you are unsure if a particular teacher or course is right for you, use your intuition to bring certainty. You can make intuitive choices from the center of your head. Use a rose to represent a teacher, course, or modality. If it looks fresh and appealing, it's a great option; if it's wilted and unappealing, it isn't. If you're choosing between multiple options, create and compare roses for each option. If you follow this guidance, it will steer you on the right path. You can even use two roses to compare doing something versus not.

CONCLUSION

Congratulations on completing the book!

My goal was to help you know yourself better, validate your intuition, and start unblocking, activating, and using it. I've provided a foundation of understanding, with tools to help on your path to become an awakened human. By grounding and centering, you can begin to unlock the book of you. You can cleanse and heal by running your energy and working with roses. As you peel away the layers, you lighten the load and increase your vibration. Then you can access more of yourself and your information than you ever imagined possible. Opening your intuition has great rewards. All your answers can be accessed through your intuition, chakras, and energy field, and by communicating with your Trusted Source. I wish you a joyful continued journey into you!

You are an eternal, multidimensional being. You are a spark of divine consciousness without a beginning or end. You will always change and find balance overall. So relax and enjoy the ride of your life. Yes, as humans we do live in a world of ups and downs. Life, in a body, can be challenging, but the techniques in this book can help your ride be smoother. You are a divine being who is part of the plan for all creation. As an awakening human with divine purpose, trusting your intuition can help you:

- answer your questions big and small
- stay on course and in alignment with source
- guide your life direction and follow your path
- heal yourself physically, mentally, and emotionally

If there is one final message I wish to convey to you it is this: Get out of your own way. When you step aside from human impulses to explain and control everything, you open to the mystery and can know the divine inside you. In knowing yourself, you also know the divine. If you build a relationship with your higher guidance, your path will be clear and your concept of reality will expand. Our lives appear linear as we experience them through time and space, and through our linear human minds. Intuition is nonlinear, multidimensional communication. It is the language of spirit. You knew it before you were born and will know it when you return to spirit. By choosing to access it now, you can become an awakened divine human.

This book contains everything you need for a complete foundation in intuition development. Yet the written word can keep us in the intellect, and it is more effective to learn through direct experience. For this reason, my gift for you is a guided meditation that will make it easier for you to activate your intuition. Listening to this recording will help you to go deeper and experience more profound results. The recording includes all the techniques taught in this book and will make it easier for you to practice them. This will help you in your daily meditation practice and ensure you continue your intuition development and spiritual growth.

Access your gift here: https://drlesleyphillips.com/intuition-and-chakras-readers-gift/.

BIBLIOGRAPHY

Bach, Richard. *Illusions: The Adventures of a Reluctant Messiah*. New York: Dell, 1989.

———. *Jonathan Livingston Seagull*. New York: Scribner, 2014.

Flora, Mary Ellen. *Chakras: Key to Spiritual Opening*. Everett: CDM Publications, 1999.

———. *Cosmic Energy: The Creative Power*. Everett: CDM Publications, 1995.

———. *Earth Energy: The Spiritual Frontier*. Everett: CDM Publications, 1996.

———. *Meditation: Key to Spiritual Awakening*. Everett: CDM Publications, 2000.

Geller, Uri, and Guy Lyon Playfair. *The Geller Effect*. New York: Henry Holt & Co., 1987.

Gober, Mark. *An End to Upside Down Thinking: Dispelling the Myth That the Brain Produces Consciousness, and the Implications for Everyday Life*. Cardiff-by-the-sea: Waterside Press, 2018.

Jeffers, Susan. *Feel the Fear and Do It Anyway*. New York: Ballantine Books, 2006.

Popp, Fritz Albert. *Integrative Biophysics: Biophotonics*. New York: Springer, 2003.

Roberts, Jane. *Seth Dreams and Projections of Consciousness*. New York: New Awareness Network, 1998.

Schucman, Helen. *A Course in Miracles: Combined Volume*. New York: Foundation for Inner Peace, 1975.

Shapiro, Joshua. *Journeys of the Crystal Skull Explorers*. Kent: Washington Crystal Skull Explorers, 2018.

Sri Swami Satchidananda. *The Yoga Sutras of Patanjali*. Buckingham: Integral Yoga Publications, 2012.

Stevenson, Ian, Zofia Weaver, and Mary Rose Barrington. *A World in a Grain of Sand: The Clairvoyance of Stefan Ossowiecki*. Jefferson, NC: McFarland & Company, 2005.

Strassman, Rick. *DMT: The Spirit Molecule: A Doctor's Revolutionary Research into the Biology of Near-Death and Mystical Experiences*. Paris: Park Street Press, 2000.

Tolle, Eckhart. *A New Earth: Awakening to Your Life's Purpose*. New York: Penguin Books, 2008.

———. *The Power of Now: A Guide to Spiritual Enlightenment*. Vancouver: Namaste Publishing, 2004.

Van Auken. John. *Edgar Cayce on the Revelation: A Study Guide for Spiritualizing Body and Mind*. New York: Sterling, 2005.

Walsch, Neale Donald. *Conversations with God, Book 4: Awaken the Species*. Faber: Rainbow Ridge Books, 2017.

To Write to the Author

If you wish to contact the author or would like more information about this book, please write to the author in care of Llewellyn Worldwide Ltd. and we will forward your request. Both the author and publisher appreciate hearing from you and learning of your enjoyment of this book and how it has helped you. Llewellyn Worldwide Ltd. cannot guarantee that every letter written to the author can be answered, but all will be forwarded. Please write to:

Lesley Phillips PhD
℅ Llewellyn Worldwide
2143 Wooddale Drive
Woodbury, MN 55125-2989

Please enclose a self-addressed stamped envelope for reply,
or $1.00 to cover costs. If outside the U.S.A., enclose
an international postal reply coupon.

Many of Llewellyn's authors have websites with additional information and resources. For more information, please visit our website at http://www.llewellyn.com.